DATE			

The Avant-Garde Today

The Avant-Garde Today

An International Anthology

Edited by
Charles Russell

University of Illinois Press
Urbana   Chicago   London

© 1981 by the Board of Trustees of the University of Illinois
Manufactured in the United States of America

Library of Congress Cataloging in Publication Data

Main entry under title:

The Avant-garde today.

1. Literature, Modern—20th century.   I. Russell, Charles, 1944–
PN6014.A9   808.8′0047   80-23922
ISBN 0-252-00851-0 (cloth)
ISBN 0-252-00852-9 (paper)

Permissions

One untitled work and "Non-denominational" by Scott Helmes; by permission of the author.

"Third Try Successful," "Gestures: A Game" by Ernst Jandl, translated by Rosmarie Waldrop; reprinted by permission of the author and translator.

"Schtzngrmm," "Chanson," "Calypso" by Ernst Jandl; reprinted by permission of the author.

"Face" by Ludovic Janvier, translated by William H. Matheson and Emma Kafalenos from *Face* (Paris: Gallimard, 1975); reprinted by permission of the author and translators.

"Color Improvisations," "C.I.A." by Toby Lurie; reprinted from *The Paris Review* 75 (1979) by permission of the author.

"I People" by Toby Lurie; by permission of the author.

"Inlet" by Clarence Major. This text appeared in altered form in *Emergency Exit* (New York: Fiction Collective), copyright © 1979 by Clarence Major; reprinted by permission of the author.

"Il Tema romantico della poesia," "Culturae," "Captivus," "Il Paesaggio falso," "Dei Gratia" by Lucia Marcucci; reprinted from *The Paris Review* 75 (1979) by permission of the author.

"Narrating of a Narration," "In a Run-Down Neighborhood," "With Each Clouded Peak" by Friederike Mayröcker, translated by Harriett Watts from *Je ein umwölkter Gipfel* (Frankfurt: Suhrkamp, 1973); reprinted by permission of the publisher and translator.

"Esse," "Rosa Rossa" by Eugenio Miccini; reprinted from *The Paris Review* 75 (1979) by permission of the author.

"Poesia," "Fuoco" by Eugenio Miccini; by permission of the author.

"Le Tre finestre/canto sospeso," "Concerto per eclisse di sole," "Corral Ouverture," "Crescendo[1] n. 1," "Narrazione Aperta" by Luciano Ori; reprinted from *The Paris Review* 75 (1979) by permission of the author.

"CodeX" by Maurice Roche, translated by Mark A. Polizzotti from *CodeX* (Paris: Seuil, 1974); by permission of the author and translator.

"Leafs," "Unite" by Gerhard Rühm, translated by Rosmarie Waldrop; by permission of the author and translator.

"Maitreya" by Severo Sarduy, translated by Suzanne Jill Levine from *Maitreya* (Barcelona: Seix Barral, 1978); reprinted by permission of the author and translator.

"Creep," "Popcrete Poem," "Counter-world" by Shimizu Toshihiko; reprinted from *The Paris Review* 75 (1979) by permission of the author.

"Eye Poem" by Shimizu Toshihiko; by permission of the author.

"Laws" by Philippe Sollers, translated by William H. Matheson and Emma Kafalenos from *Lois* (Paris: Seuil, 1972); reprinted by permission of the author and translators.

"Text for 'to'," "Information Sculpture," "Poems Fall," by Takahashi Shohachiro; reprinted from *The Paris Review* 75 (1979) by permission of the author.

"Poems Fall" by Takahashi Shohachiro; by permission of the author.

"Forest Poem," "Building Piece," and "About Memory" by Jiri Valoch; reprinted by permission of the author.

"Anniversary Date of Rubens," "Notting Hill" by Paul de Vree; reprinted from *The Paris Review* 75 (1979) by permission of the author.

"Nothing Has Changed," "Numbers," "The Street Tells the Truth" by Paul de Vree; reprinted by permission of the author.

Contents

Acknowledgments

My efforts to compile this anthology benefited from the support and assistance of several individuals, most notably Alain Arias-Misson, who helped contact a number of the writers whose works I wished to include and whose suggestions and enthusiasm were always appreciated. George Plimpton and the staff of *The Paris Review* were supportive through the various stages of this project. Many of these works were published in a portfolio, "Word and Image," which I edited for the Spring, 1979, issue of *The Paris Review*. Most important, however, was the initial encouragement of John Rowlett, who suggested—what now seems like ages ago—the need for a collection and commentary such as *The Avant-Garde Today*.

Introduction

1

A Short History
of the Term *Avant-Garde*

ca.

1794— A military term designating the elite shock troops of the French army, whose mission was to initially engage the enemy in order to prepare the way for the main body of troops to follow.

ca.

1830— A political concept current among utopian socialists. Used as early as 1825 by the Saint-Simonian writer Olinde Rodrigues and later by Fourier's disciple Laverdant, the term *avant-garde* was applied to the "men of vision" of the coming society—artists, philosophers, scientists, and businessmen—whose actions would direct the future development of humanity.

ca.

1870— An aesthetic metaphor commonly used to identify successive movements of writers and artists who, within the larger cultural framework of modernism, were intent on dramatically establishing their own formal conventions in distinct opposition to the reigning academic or popular taste. The radically disruptive and visionary writings of Lautréamont and Rimbaud gave birth to the literary avant-garde in the late 1860's. By the 1870's, art critics utilized the term to describe the innovations of Manet and the early impressionists. During the next seventy years—and particularly from 1910 through 1930, the high point of the avant-garde—the term signified those literary and artistic movements (Expressionism, Russian and Italian Futurism, Dada, Surrealism, Constructivism, etc.) whose simultaneous culturally antagonistic and visionary impulses generated a vital tradition of social radicalism and aesthetic innovation.

ca.
1968— A convenient label applied to the postwar reemergence of self-conscious stylistic innovation in the arts. The formal indebtedness of pop, minimal, and conceptual art to the past avant-garde, particularly to Dada and the spirit of Duchamp, as well as the self-reflexive novel's evident apprenticeship to the great modernists such as Joyce and Beckett led some critics to speak of a "neo-avant-garde" and to criticize the apparent "academicism" of the avant-garde. However, in literature, at least, the works of writers as diverse as Cortazar, Pynchon, Barthelme, Grass, Robbe-Grillet, Reed, and Handke were clearly not simple expressions of narrow literary tradition; rather, they reflected the widespread cultural disruption and political struggles of the 1960's and early 1970's. These writers' works, while frequently apolitical, were part of a larger questioning of this culture's values and stability. And even though these authors were soon grouped under still another historical category—the postmodern—and though the dissipation of radical energies in the 1970's left the literary avant-garde without a sustaining model of social transformation, much of recent avant-garde experimentation has displayed a continued social questioning and has attempted to alter the means of individual and collective perception, expression, and perhaps behavior.

1981— The avant-garde today remains with us as a sanctioned aesthetic predilection, if not an institution. It suggests a personal and social need for renovation, for potentiality, change, and freedom. Struggling within the confines of a self-reflexive formal orientation and against an ill-defined social context of liberal and diffusive pluralism, the avant-garde bears curious witness to an ambiguous state of mind. It displays a creative and critical vitality, yet raises only minimal expectations. It countenances an active and often aggressive assertion of individual will, yet betrays an uneasy acquiescence and resignation. Its most significant innovations involve the self-conscious exploration of the nature, limits, and possibilities of literature in contemporary society. But the vision of the future of this literature and culture which the avant-garde works should provide is tentative and unclear, as if the avant-garde could not lead beyond doubt and distrust toward inspired vision.

5

2

The Avant-Garde in the Postmodern Era

What does it mean to be avant-garde today? What vision of art and society does this literature of experimentation and innovation reveal? What social and literary significance can the avant-garde claim in contemporary culture?

This collection of European, Japanese, and American avant-garde texts attempts to provide some answers to these questions. The pieces presented here represent the thematic concerns and formal innovations that characterize the work of the avant-garde during the past two decades. The collection is not meant to be comprehensive, for certainly there are many other writers now working who could be called avant-garde (just as some here might reject the label). Indeed, the dynamics of the avant-garde are such that by the time a writer is sufficiently established to be included in an anthology such as this, there must surely be a new generation of avant-garde writers emerging to claim attention in the future. Several of the writers included here are well established and have been influencing the avant-garde movement for more than twenty years; others, known in their own countries, have received inadequate recognition in the United States; still others have only begun to have their works appear in print.

Most of these texts are from Europe and the United States. Avant-garde experimentation remains strong in Europe, especially in France, Germany and Italy, because of the continent's tradition of sophisticated political analysis and continuing social unrest, as well as the legacy of the many avant-garde movements which blossomed there during the first half of this century. In the United States recent literary innovation has been generated largely by the concurrent growth, during the 1960's, of an active middle-class art market and audience (which similarly influenced the visual arts, music, theater, and dance) and the cultural rebellion of the young. The avant-garde is developing, however, in other parts of the world as well. In South America, much of contemporary poetry is clearly overshadowed by the previous generations of poets such as Neruda, Paz and Vallejo. And while the remarkable development of South American fiction proves it to be the most vital writing in the world today, many of the recent novels represent a marriage of established, European modernist aesthetics with an interest in indigenous history and myth. This combination results in startlingly imaginative narratives, but as yet few works display the avant-garde compulsion to break free from history and past convention in order to seek a radically different future. Nevertheless, innovative work is being done by writers such as Sarduy, Infante, and Cortazar, whose frequent periods of residence in Europe place them in close contact with contemporary avant-garde movements. In Japan, the growth of an avant-garde spirit is one expression of postwar industrialization and westernization, as well as a sign of the recent entry of Japanese writers into the international literary and artistic communities.

It should be evident from this anthology that there is not just one avant-garde today, but many. However, while showing the often radical differences among these writers, I hope to point out the similarities of interest and situation that unite them and give focus to the contemporary avant-garde. In particular, this book focuses on these writers' radical explorations of their means of expression—the forms, functions, limits, and possibilities inherent in the act of writing—and on that act's ambiguous and often antagonistic relationship to the language and meaning systems, the values and ideology of contemporary culture.

It is important to note from the start the close connections between the aesthetic concerns and social context of the writers presented here and those of postmodernists such as Barth, Robbe-Grillet, Borges, Coover, Vonnegut, Marquez, and Kosinski, to name but a few. For the avant-garde is a phenomenon which must be seen in relation to the broader cultural developments of its society. Just as the earlier avant-garde was an offshoot of, but antagonistic to, the dominant literary and artistic movement of modernism, the postwar avant-garde is a particular (if extreme) form of the contemporary cultural spirit known as the postmodern.

The boundaries between the recent avant-garde and postmodernism are perhaps more difficult to determine than those between the earlier avant-garde and modernism since, like the old avant-garde, postmodernism itself undermines modernist assumptions—especially modernism's cultural elitism and political conservatism, its belief in the privileged status of literary language, and its search for a transcendent or ahistorical dimension of human experience. Nevertheless, the avant-garde today sustains its predecessor's strident insistence on the primary importance of radical experimentation with the materials of art, and it displays a compulsion to question and possibly change the very basis of personal and cultural articulation. While these programs may be related to postmodernism's general focus on the materials and structures of literary artifice, and to its frequent creation of self-reflexive literary fabulations, the avant-garde emphasizes instead the more disruptive, perhaps liberating, and in many cases inherently political aspects of its linguistic experiments. For example, rather than following the innovative strategies of postmodernists such as Barth, Borges, and Robbe-Grillet, who insist on the fictive nature of all experience known through language and who consequently offer primarily internal explorations of the experience of literature as self-reflexive artifice, the avant-garde struggles to make the text point beyond such encapsulation—beyond the established patterns of literary expression toward the as yet unformulated, unspoken, and unknown, beyond itself toward the newly appearing texture of personal experience, or beyond the hermeticism of literature toward the complex workings of collective discourse and behavior.

Within postmodernism, of course, there are writers such as Pynchon, Coover, and Fuentes, who also move beyond the self-imposed aesthetic restrictions to link the self-reflexive patterns of their narratives to the collective frameworks of history or myth, or who highlight the limitations of personal and literary language within the context of established social systems of ideology and power. But the writers presented in this collection push the self-reflexive disruption of language to extremes, at times distorting narrative structure, syntax, even the forms of words and letters, to force the text and language, the writer and reader into new patterns of perception and expression. Gambling against incomprehensibility, even illegibility, such an aesthetic raises the most problematic questions of personal and literary expression and for some, by extension, opens up new perspectives on social experience. Therefore, the particular focus of this book is on the explicit questions that the avant-garde raises about itself and the practice of writing in our time, and consequently, on the questions that we, the audience, must ask about this society and its literature.

The book is arranged thematically. The first section, "The Personal Context," emphasizes the nature and limits of our personal perspectives in society and in writing. It inquires into how the contemporary avant-garde limns the interaction of self and external world: how the world is perceived, known, acted upon, and described; and similarly, how we apprehend and respond to the effect of the world on us. The second section, "Discourse and Experiment," extends this questioning to the process of writing, focusing in particular on the nature of and reasons for the radical linguistic self-reflexiveness that distinguishes so much of the avant-garde today. It asks about the relationship between literary language and common usage, and examines an individual's freedom and restrictions in shaping, distorting, or transforming that most collective of phenomena—language. The third, "The Social Text," refers us to the continuing tradition of avant-garde extremism and social radicalism. It discusses the interaction of self and language as the basis of understanding the social and ideological implications of our placement within social discourse and values. It asks, for example: To what extent does the avant-garde today sustain a political dimension? Toward what future does it point?

These three topics are not, of course, mutually exclusive. It is neither possible nor desirable to separate completely an individual's sense of personal definition from his or her response to the social environment; nor can we isolate a writer's manipulation of literary conventions from literature's connections to its culture's prevailing linguistic usage. Consequently, some of the writers in this book are presented in more than one section, with particular works chosen to illustrate the developing argument in this anthology.

The structure of the general argument provides an expanding frame of reference, from the personal to the collective; at the same time, it suggests an implied progression from personal ambiguity and passivity toward cultural analysis and activism. But that activism, as we shall see, remains a peculiarly tentative and often unfocused affair. For the doubt, pain, paranoia, and even despair reflected in the personal context are never fully transcended by the more visionary dimensions of the avant-garde.

Part I

The Personal Context

3

The Uneasy Activism
of the Avant-Garde

What does it mean to be avant-garde today? To be "in advance"? In advance of what?

Traditionally, the avant-garde expresses a historical sensibility. A future-oriented art, it declares its faith in the necessary transformation of art, consciousness, and society. It is known as both nihilistic and visionary: antagonistic toward whatever inhibits change, activist in its attempt to stimulate change. It is an art of discovery, of innovation and experimentation. Its goal is the expansion of consciousness and the liberation of behavior. The common assumption of all avant-gardes is that new forms of perception and expression lead to new states of consciousness and action. Implicit in all avant-garde manifestoes are these corollary beliefs:

The act of discovery is an agent of liberation.

The act of liberation is an agent of discovery.

As an activist art, the avant-garde is inherently political. It implies that the aesthetic act has social significance and, furthermore, that aesthetic activism either supports or is an expression of existing social forces of change. From its very beginning, the avant-garde has sought to identify such forces, either political or scientific, which might generate a cultural transformation of which experimental art could be an agent. Rimbaud's personal identification with the commune of 1871 and his bohemian scorn for bourgeois conventions, Apollinaire's fascination with technological advances as signs of the future development of society, Italian

Futurism's jingoist and proto-fascist idolatry of technology, the military and financial power, Zurich Dada's radical pacifism and nihilism, Berlin Dada's communist sympathies, Mayakovsky's and Russian Futurism's efforts to link aesthetic innovation to the needs of post-revolutionary society, Surrealism's attempt to place art at the service of the revolution, even Brecht's transformation of the conventions of the theater to promote in his audience a socially critical perspective—all of these express the avant-garde's spirit of social and aesthetic activism. These writers and movements believed themselves to be integral elements of historical change. During periods of political and social disruption (World War I, the 1920's, the 1960's), the avant-garde tends to accent its political dimension as it attempts to connect individual experience and innovation to a broader social context. During times of social ambivalence or conformity, more hermetic models of analysis and change are emphasized, for in these eras the individual writer feels most strongly the burden of sustaining the radical vision alone.

Such a social ambivalence and analytic aesthetic characterize the avant-garde today. Though influenced by the worldwide political unrest of the 1960's, the literature of the past decade has been primarily the expression of a period of retrenchment. The abstract and self-reflexive strategies of both postmodernism and the recent avant-garde signal sharply circumscribed aesthetic visions. Their nearly exclusive focus on the laws of semiotic systems contributes to the avant-garde's retreat from its former behavioral radicalism. Today the nature of its activism—its effort to act directly on the determinants of perception, cognition, and articulation—is governed by the assumption that all behavior (including alternate visions of reality, whether personal, literary, or political) is first and foremost mediated through language and that, consequently, the "scientific" analysis of language and direct self-reflexive action within it are the first priorities of the avant-garde text.

Many of the experimental works in this collection may at first appear to be impenetrable, gratuitous, or overly self-indulgent. Frequently the social dimension does not exist, or is only allusively suggested. Nevertheless, the constant emphasis on formal innovation and on personal and social semiotic analysis suggests an abiding belief in the necessity and possibility of change in society's discourse, or initially, at least, in its art. And though many of these self-proclaiming texts may owe much to the by now traditional posturing of the avant-garde sensibility, they still express the dynamics of an art and a society imbued with a faith in unceasing historical change.

The avant-garde and its audience must ask whether this sense of change presages a significant cultural development. We need determine what historical vision the avant-garde can be expected to project. What models for radical social change exist today? What forces within our organized, post-industrial capitalist state might generate a meaningful development of human potential? In which areas of our society can the dream of creative freedom flourish? Finally, these questions must refer back to literature's audience. How do this society's citizens—not merely its writers—perceive themselves and their future? What potential for change and what restrictions exist in our culture? What promise? What threat?

4

The Ambiguity of Personal Perspective

What promise? What threat? Haunting the avant-garde, these two questions. At the heart of the avant-garde, an ambiguity. The innovative writer faces an ill-defined aesthetic and social dilemma of both apparent freedom and sensed restriction. The avant-garde today affirms its aesthetic and behavioral play, its free experimentation and constant innovation, all within an environment and to an audience which readily accepts, even if not universally acclaiming, its existence. But at the same time, this play, rather than being perceived as a celebration of the potential of human life, is often felt to be irrelevant to, or perhaps merely an avoidance of, the primary concerns of our social existence.

Contemporary literature, both postmodern and avant-garde, is dominated by feelings of both paranoia and freedom. In fact, the two sensations are conflicting expressions of a single situation. In the works of the avant-garde writers in this collection as well as in those of postmodernists such as Pynchon, Robbe-Grillet, Barthelme, and Handke, we constantly encounter paranoid characters and situations. The characters and their authors assert the benefits of a strident individualism and, having little apparent connection to the world about them, try desperately to create and shape their own space of freedom and self-definition. But most must face the suggestion that they may actually have little or no control over their lives. Rather, it is hinted, they are controlled and molded by forces beyond direct observation; their freedom is just a delusion. Because those forces are rarely made visible, much less identified, the sense of apparent freedom remains strong. The central issue is, then, to determine one's limits or one's scope of action and freedom—and to distinguish what shapes those alternatives.

The tensions of freedom and restriction, of promise and threat, are particularly evident within the immediate personal context. They manifest themselves in two sets of mutually dependent yet antagonistic polarities: individualism/homogenization, and fragmentation/totalization. From the perspective of the writer and the creative act, our lives seem to profit from an unrestrained freedom. Individualism appears to flourish amid liberal pluralism. But at the same time, we can sense our enclosure within an increasingly homogenous culture, a mass society of limited behavioral options that effectively denies significant personal differentiation. And if we are able to transcend an individualistic perspective, personal freedom appears to be but a form of fragmentation, of isolation and alienation within determining patterns of cultural, behavioral, or ideological structures more restrictive than the felt immediacy of that freedom would suggest.

The challenge we face is finally that of accurate perception and interpretation of the world around us, and of the ideas, values, and languages that influence us. It is particularly significant that semiotics—the "science" of the analysis of signs and the interaction of meaning systems—dominates the contemporary social sciences, humanities, and arts. Writers and critics today argue that we are surrounded by culturally determined signs and meaning systems, languages which we speak and which shape our utterances. To perceive, act, speak, or write, every action necessitates a self-reflexive analysis if it is to claim individual integrity. For there are messages all around us, waiting—demanding—to be interpreted; more often than not, the message announces the diminishing realm of personal freedom. Just beyond clear perception or seemingly adequate language there is some essential promise or threat that must be understood.

The apparent peace and order that envelop us belie a tension, a conflict that is barely suppressed. Who or what threatens and limits perception, knowledge, action? The postmodern and avant-garde writers raise these questions and respond with a series of tentative probes—probes of the given and the desired, of personal authority and social pressure, of language and the imagination. For the avant-garde writer especially, such probing leads to extreme forms of rebellion against cultural authority and abstraction, against established social reality and its literary formulations. In the process, language and the way we speak are questioned, disrupted, distorted, even denied. Each avant-garde text in some manner brings language to the fore, in order to see the relationship between what is spoken and how it is said, between what is perceived and how it is presented. The search is to determine what controls our lives, our speech, our actions. And with this search inevitably come both optimism and paranoia, be they comic or desperate.

In the following texts by Helmut Heissenbüttel, the search is abortive. Experience is fraught with messages. The phenomenal world is animated and hints at some mystery. But direct insight into the occurrences and mysteries eludes us. Voices fall into patterns of repetition and tautology, and ultimately are reduced to a few not very satisfying sentences which betray a mood of quiet resignation.

The speakers in Jürgen Becker's novel are similarly overwhelmed by the plethora of unsorted data, desires, memories, events, and questions. Everything they encounter proves equally meaningful and equally banal, since all is reduced to a common denominator of uncritical transcription. Yet a definite note of disorientation and despair is present, and a lost security is regretted, only to be sought in a set of clichés that prove as meaningless as everything else in their universe.

For Alain Arias-Misson, the messages that may be hidden from people or that they may embrace within themselves are all too visible to those around them. Signs of despair, anger, need, and arrogance, the detritus of desire and the graffiti of feelings all form an unspoken but universal message.

Helmut Heissenbüttel

dark figures write the script I understand too late
obscene clothesracks undress behind my back
the monologue of the cranes on the evening sky spells disaster
scraps of paper flee breathless through areas of rubbish
rain makes itself understood with splashrhythms
the steps in the hallway form silent knots
the wind of the lanterns is afraid
telling joints of fear
fading into the slowly collapsing window
the gap between the clouds uncovers its own handwriting
nobody recognizes the lampshades feeling their way
sometimes I'm in hell and sometimes in heaven
nobody recognizes the zigzag of the shadows in the window
fading into the slowly collapsing window the blackboard
the spinning of the blackboard

   —trans. Rosmarie Waldrop

Simple Grammatical Meditations

a [tautologies]
the shadow I cast is the shadow I cast
the situation I got into is the situation I got into
the situation I got into is yes and no
situation my situation my particular situation
groups of groups move across empty planes
groups of groups move across pure colors
groups of groups move across the shadow I cast
the shadow I cast is the shadow I cast
groups of groups move across the shadow I cast and disappear

b
the black of the water and the points of light
the black of the water and the random reflections
regions and regions and landscapes
landscapes I've colored and landscapes I haven't colored
the random shadows and the chromatic brightness
the blackness of the black and the chromatic bright spots
yellow red redyellow and red red red
regions and landscapes and or
or and or or

c [subjunctive]
up to the middle of half
less than too little
least
as if as if
probably probably
taken on not taken on
undecided
preliminary preliminary

d
shadings of reflections and mirrorings and afternoons
afternoons and afternoons and afternoons
afternoons are more customary than pasts
afternoons are no more frequent than pasts
the afternoon with which I name is more namable than pasts
slowly removed afternoons through a shading of reflections
advanced advances refer
cracked mirrors and more cracked afternoons
more cracked afternoons and more cracked afternoons

e
small black verticals cross slow black horizontals
raininess crosses raininess
crowds of walls
small black sad incessantly wandering rectangles
hesitant diagonals
crossing straight finite lines
in any case in a given case and I talk talk
talk crosses talk and there is there is there not not
talk crosses talk and there is there is there not not and
        never never

f [participial]
to waitingly wait have waited
to be waited
to have been won over not won over won over
revoked revocations
sounds stretched crosswise
sounds stretched crosswise from finite points of time
revoked revocations pending revocation directing towards
erect directed towards erected direction
erect direction from infinite points of time

—trans. Rosmarie Waldrop

22

simple sentences
while I stand the shadow falls
morning sun sketches the first design
flowering is a deadly business
I have agreed
I live

—trans. Rosmarie Waldrop

23

The Underground Again

Apocalypse

Obituaries

Jürgen Becker

From *Margins*

Here hangs the map; all walls are white; this is the country; these are the coasts; this is history; that is the tall window with the trees in the park; above, the sky; this is our daily DC-8; that is our cat Nina; today is Friday; no summer; no change; this is the past heartbeat; here the something called hope returns; this is the time it takes to smoke a cigarette; a deadline approaches; this is Münchhausen dragging a wild boar behind him; this is the nearness of what is talked about; the name Mila Schön is mentioned; this must be Milano; the full glass; the empty glass; somebody sits there, sits at the table looking up from the tabletop; there something else; this is the Inner Continent; this is it, clean as an Opel from Opel; there hangs Kaiser Wilhelm, red plaster; there it's 10 PM and there it's 8 AM; the fly over there isn't flying; this is the important point; this is what you forget; this is the Mississippi; this is the word which designates the river; there is an empty, cold stove, there is a good transistor radio, there and there a piece of column each, there something to sit on and there something to sit and lie on.

And outside, the storm whips through the area; and a swarm of birds struggles till dark.

What may happen tomorrow: the mail may not come and yesterday's letter still be in the box. Schnellinger may visit a compatriot. The wind may shift. Reason to go back to bed. Nina may go out again and not come back. A strike in Italy. Ideas which don't bring in money. The return of Raquel Welch. Always more interruptions. A pilot may get drunk and fall asleep. The president's wife may go for a walk. We may foul up and start over. Driving to the supermarket together. Buying a new shirt. Death. Six cups of tea. A marvelous horoscope for the day after tomorrow. The Chinese at the door. A call from Ingeborg in the rain. We may have forgotten it all again and think we've seen it all before.

Going for a drive. Gets us back into good spirits. The flat countryside is almost altogether devastated. An often scenic route connects the many, typical scenic views and allows us to circle the lake. In the midst of the white wasteland we find a white hotel where we spend the night awake. Whoever falls asleep is never seen again. Close behind the mountains there ought to be the sea with the harbor which means safety. In a guidebook we read about the people who have only one leg and whose one foot is so large that they can lie in its shade and be sheltered from the burning sun. Our tongues are swollen, our feet full of thorns and swelling up. Seeing the Acapulco beauties makes us forget either. This lake used to be a crater. A few miles before Anguillara, two tall pines stand to the left and right of the road through the enormous plain. Toward noon, we stop at the inn whose owner is just washing off the blood. In the next town, many children are dancing to a flute. The plain is larger than we thought. There, a village, and there another, and there is one burning. Smaller and smaller the cattle, the woods, the earth. We promise to keep silent. Since the gate fell shut behind us, we stand in the night. The next morning, up early and first thing out into the middle of the lake. The clouds above the mountains don't augur well. We strain our eyes. There is the car. Right, we lack water and air. Air does not boil over, nor does it freeze. We find a river bed and are happy about this way to safety. Then we see the capital of the province. Some railroad stations, army drilling grounds, a formerly thriving commerce, the Main Residence of the Prince, shot guards, bathing huts, the plague cemetery, Herbert Street, a museum which used to be an enemy camp, some catacombs, a dozen monuments, a lot of thistles and other weeds, some footprints, any number of lizards, several houses in good condition. Tired and happy, we return home in the evening. Many guests have already arrived, and we tell about our trip to the province.

Some names in the order of remembering the events.
Divorce. M. grins through his tears.
September, Hannes, near Campi.

Ludovica Nagel introduces Monica Vitti.

My name is Hans Stahl.

S. Ubway, like SUBWAY.

Flirting, always flirting, said Herr Dvelius.

When it was said the Americans were here Karlchen Tümmler put on his white chef's hat.

Paffrath, the good humor man over there?

Huth, said Hofer, said Huth, said Sotrop.

Herr Zimmermann, ah yes, Herr Zimmermann.

Finally Hilde showed her passport and there couldn't be any more doubt.

Take care, said Liesbeth.

Fritz Herkenrath catches the ball.

September 1950 in Dellbrück had as much mist and mellow fruitfulness as Keats' Autumn.

Boris asks his father why he won't come back.

Stan Kenton ice-grey.

Even Lilo suddenly looked changed.

When they fell down, one after the other, Panna Grady only smiled ironically.

Pyla had already taken a taxi.

The wind turns. Hausmann wears his baseball cap with the bill in back.

Adrion makes a coin disappear.

Andy Warhol sat there calmly as the noise grew louder and louder.

Natascha Ungeheuer.

First he said his name was unpronounceable. Then he gave a false name. At dinner, he claimed to live under a pseudonym. Helen Stauffachler simply couldn't believe all this.

Happel.

Shortly before moving out of Anna Street, Walter once more wrecked the apartment.

We are still arguing if Sandra got into the little or the big Fiat.

And why not?

Because elsewhere everything starts over. Because my back hurts. Because it's raining. Because the conductor said it comes to the same thing. Because you don't want to yourself. Because nobody will show up anyway. Because I simply can't stand it anymore. Because it's too late and nobody said anything. Because he didn't hold still. Because then we'll finally have peace. Because nobody knows about it so far. Because it turned out it doesn't work either. Because you always make such a fuss. Because it's always the same thing and because everybody says it'll change. Because nothing ever changes. Because nothing more was said about it today, no, even yesterday. Because you simply can't lay into them nowadays. Because nothing worthwhile is going on. Because it's again the same people. Because nobody goes along with it and because it stinks. Because there's no reason to be for or against it. Because I don't care. Because it's still raining. Because otherwise you'll leave. Because it'll all stop by itself.

. . .

It starts right after breakfast. An hour later it is still three. During the next hour two more. Little peace till noon. Noon, finally. After lunch it really gets going. One and none is all one. Come on, let's go to the park. The park air is fresh and healthy. It's never too late to start afresh. A fresh start.
Fresh struggle at the table. Defeat, Despair. Once more from the beginning. Up from the table, to the couch, into the armchair, around the table, at the table again. Can't stand on one leg for long—so another one. Life is hard enough as it is. And not too much pleasure in it. What for anyway? All good things come, well what number do they come in?
Contrite at supper. How many did I have. Now there are visitors on top of it all, well it's a change, greetings, pleasure, hello. Everybody stands around, loose, relaxed, and why not, everybody has tried it out and knows how it's done, no more thinking about it, and we all die one way or another. You too, and all of them as they are. Open the window. A clear night. Breathe deeply. Then start coughing in the bathroom. Tomorrow, a new leaf: no more smoking.

When it started there was no way of telling what it was all about. When the time had come everybody said it's a good thing that the time has come. When it continued, of course, the first difficulties cropped up. When it suddenly came to a halt, one thing and another was tried until it went on again. And when it got so it worked rather well, nobody had anything against it.

Why don't you go on.

Well, and when nothing interfered, nobody thought any more about it.

When, later, a few little things happened, well, after all, who pays that much attention to the little details. When it got worse, people got thoughtful. But when it became clear what was the matter, how could anybody do anything about it. When it was suddenly a real mess, everybody had other things to think about. Then, when it was all over, it really looked very different from what everybody had thought at the beginning. Because when it started there was no way of telling what it was all supposed to be about. Only when the time had come, only then did everybody say it's really a good thing that the time has come. True, as it continued, the first difficulties started to crop up right away. But when it suddenly came to a halt, everything was tried until it went on again. And when it got so it worked for rather a long time, no, really, nobody had anything against it.

Why don't you go on.

And when it was long over and forgotten, there were the first tries to start it all over again.

. . .

Dark today, dreary, dull and desolate. Everything halting and heavy. So sodden, so slow. Everything dragging on. Nothing starting, nothing going on, it's no use, nothing helps, there's no sun, neither in the sky nor in your heart. Everything's loud, cold, dumb, blinding, it's no good. It's no fun, it gets on my nerves, it's killing me, it's unspeakable. No, it's nothing new, it can't be explained, it won't stop, it's everywhere. It just wreaks your head, you can't breathe, your eyes hurt, it's all empty, it's nothing. It's this restlessness, it's so hot, it's terribly bright, it just wears you out, it goes racing on and on. The time won't move, no breath of air, nothing stirs, and the noise, the flickering. And nobody gets up and says it right out that everything is dull today, so cold, so still, and that nobody can stand it any more.

A new visitor is announced. From Munich, they say, Bavaria, no longer young, no longer dangerous, doesn't eat much, drinks moderately, won't stay long either, knows only stories from the good old days, forgets any insult, is said to smile when you throw him out, appreciates everything, doesn't ask questions, mostly invisible, won't cause messes, tried to assassinate somebody, but long ago, knew the king, recites ballads if asked, doesn't really like to come, said somewhere he's a little afraid of us, already called it off a couple of times, called it off again today.

. . .

New knowledge:
The visitor who just arrived is not at all the one who was announced.
Nina, the cat, is pregnant.
Five London shops have opened in a Rome backstreet.
Too much, last night, too much.
Last year around this time it was much warmer.
Arndt has inherited his greatgrandfather's unfortunate character.
It wasn't as bad as all that.
The cat population of Rome is estimated at 120,000.
When somebody shows up and says come along, we don't feel like it, and when we feel like coming along if somebody would show up and say come along, then nobody comes and says come along.
There's always suffering somewhere.
The pope is the pope.
The new Dino is quite a hot rod.
If everything is done right, the second head grows on all right.
Never before was youth this young.
Aha. This is what happened to Faruk.
Hunting season's here.
The novel is alive and well.

In the old days everything was different. The towns were larger, and the villages still villages. In the old days there was still justice, and if you didn't learn you got it beaten into you. Our teachers were still the same as our parents' teachers. Sundays we still wore our Sunday best. The lid was still on the pot, and the watch on the Rhine. In the old days, we knew God was on our side. In the old days, Hans Muff would come. Whoever was caught was put to the stake. The summers were real summers. Vacations seemed endless. Milk was still wholesome. In the old days we knew what was what. People still hiked. People who spent their time in bars would end up doing time in jail. In the old days people still walked. People protected their parks. Not like nowadays. There were still enemies where you could see the whites of their eyes. Wherever you went you could find people with the same ideas. Those who didn't know any better kept their mouths shut, and those who couldn't fit in no way went to the blazes. In the old days there were still niggers, spics, and chinks. In the old days everything was much simpler. This sort of thing would never happen. None of all this. In the old days people still listened when people talked of the old days.

They just sit around, all over the place, on the steps, on the fences, on the car roofs, on the beach, in the woods, they won't even budge if you kick them.

Quick, forget everything, right away.

One look at a town, on to the next, not cither, so on to the third, again nothing, on, maybe another one, just move on.

All obstacles removed, we can start, start, all day long we say start.

. . .

A few questions:
Are you happier now?
Is father flying in this plane?
Why did it all happen this way?
What will we do in September when the money's gone?
What's the matter with John and the others?

Why do all your marriages break up?
Barthelme, why doesn't anybody read Barthelme?
Whom would you rather have: the Fascists or the Chinese?
What are a biochemist, a city planner, and a forester doing at IBM?
Is this really the right way?
Who will stop first?
Have we at least learned something?
Would you like to be, say, ten years younger?
Who on earth are all these people running back and forth on the gravel?
Who ever tells you anything that helps you on a bit?

This place, no, it's not our place. We're not at home here, nor are we guests. We are here and won't stay forever. Beautiful days, often. The winter harder than we thought. Once we meant to describe the place, but orientation weakens, the eye clouds over; also too much chaos, too many stage sets, no memories here, more and more every man is an island, no more love, no more question of it. Sometimes you want to run away screaming. Why are we here? We don't even think about it anymore, as long as we live in reasonable comfort. What about the old country? People here just shut their ears. Once you're outside you stay outside, they say. Nobody goes mad here, because memory sleeps too damn well. Yes, we sleep away half the day. At night we have fun. Even the grumbling goes down although there's always reason. The usual guests don't bark or bite. We have nothing to tell. Sometimes we get very confused. What we think we are seeing disappears. A rustle inside your head. Erased world. Proverb time. Life with maps. There is California. Where is our place? Not here, and not here either, but there, over there we'd like to go, and there too. Time's gone by again, and again we've forgotten. Mornings it's worst. It takes a while till we know again where we are, what we'll do, where we'll go. Vague, the things we say. Wasn't any different in the old days: at the end of the vague days it all started over again. But we really like to take trips and we'll get around to describing a few. Yesterday we went to the beach. There, in the sand, we lay sleeping until the wind pushed clouds over the sun. The cold doesn't kill here. The place doesn't kill. Yes, where there's been so much history nothing happens, everything has already happened. We say to-day. Today is not the Friday we started out on. And the place where we are sitting is a long way off.

—trans. Rosmarie Waldrop

Alain Arias-Misson

St. Valentine's

Chapeau! à mon compatriôte René

God

5

Visions of Violence
and Exploitation

Paranoia, pain, doubt, and confusion dominate the personal context as individuals seek to understand the nature of their experience. Not surprisingly, these emotions frequently escalate into stark fear or disgust, as the writers perceive not only how little control they have over their lives, but also how often those lives and the lives around them turn ugly. The social determinants of the personal context are never absent. Indeed, the two often appear to be indistinguishable extensions of each other. The horror that surrounds individuals enters and distorts their personal lives and binds them to the environment. Conversely, their own anguish, fears, and desires are projected upon the social backdrop, which seems at times to be only the lurid expression of solipsistic nightmares. Even if the precise connections between self and environment are not to be determined, the threat of imminent violence, whether from within or without, goads individuals into grasping at proffered versions of reality which seem to offer stability and protection but which prove to be only further expressions of the confusion.

Common to the literary works that depict this situation is an ever oscillating focus. Unable to present a detached and omnipotent perspective, the texts alternately offer images of localized sharp focus and passages of referential vagueness. Scenes of direct violence stand out, but seem deracinated from recognizable surroundings. We perceive images of brutal clarity amid backgrounds of confusion and mystery. Parts are taken for wholes; wholes disintegrate into parts. Yet out of it all, out of this literature of fragmentation, a message seeks to make itself understood.

In Clarence Major's "Inlet," we encounter just such a series of deracinated, fragmentary, yet brutally vivid images, scenes of faded dreams and desires, of exploitation, oppression, absurdity, and violence. Ceaselessly shifting in focus and style, the text moves from naturalism to surrealism and back with no apparent logic; yet, most disturbingly, the shifts nevertheless seem all too natural within the landscape he describes.

This fragment from Ludovic Janvier's *Face* offers a nightmare vision of a voyeur's passive-aggressive fantasies of sadism, masochism, lust, and violence, fantasies evidently received from and at the same time projected upon a movie screen by the viewer. Private fantasy becomes collective dream; collective myth rules personal behavior. But in spite of the violence and eroticism they seek, the viewers remain distinctly passive, anesthetized consumers of their own mystifications.

Amiri Baraka recognizes the duplicity of the "reality" that is projected on the screen (here, a television screen). What is beamed at us in the name of reality, he declares, is a deluding fiction, but a fiction which ironically reveals the stark truth about the culture that sells and consumes those fictions—if we only choose to see. Here again, on screen and off, violence informs our lives; but the violence is diffuse, and the patterns of omnipresent exploitation can easily be avoided. Anesthetization is a distinct possibility—it seems, in fact, to be the general condition. But in the wind, in the declining days and seasons of this culture a scream, an action, a rebellion begin to grow.

Clarence Major

Inlet

They fed that possessed woman ice cream and cake her body was swollen fifty or sixty people sucked at her mouth and vagina and anus and nose and eyes. Things were nasty out there in that vacant lot where she lay on a rusty cot.

After twelve hours she gave them a loud fart and they all went home.

She died from cancer anyway and was reborn ten years later as a nurse in Bloomfield New Jersey working the night shift.

Now the boys line up at the soda fountain trying to remember what it was they wanted to do. Dreamy look in the eye. Blue leather jacket. Thin lips quivering. A thug. The music is straight out of cheeseburger heaven the boys dream of a rose in Spanish Harlem of skyscrapers greenlit backrooms of pool players sharp as tacks Tina Turner making that sucking sound of snatch of being a lonesome fugitive of strawberry hills and fields forever of Salley as she goes around the roses of rebels of the guitar man of Brenda Lee of Claudette of shooting a man in Reno of honkytonk angels of stealing a car of getting laid in the back seat of a car of turning into a werewolf of getting drunk of . . .

"Hard work and clean living my folks came here my grandparents the Quakers the Indians the Puritans nobody knows the troubles you get your reward in . . .violence well you see in them days news didn't get about so fast so we've been here since the cow jumped over the moon."

Joe who takes care of the mules has not looked into the face of another person in over thirty years.

"Great Savings Through Superior Pussy." Now I was the only one among us who sternly opposed that pitch the factory the warehouse the main office were in up-roar. Trudy designed the catalogue of artificial vaginas and she suggested another approach . . .

We sell directly. Direct distribution results in our remarkable low prices. The ones with hair on them and the real smell and warmth we have sold to kings and queens and princes and princesses and congressmen and dictators and . . .

Branches in . . .

Observe also no minimum order is required from persons who purchase their pussies in person we also carry a complete line of penises but that is not my department . . .

We can assure we are working for the space age the United States of America and its Territories sincerely yours Superior Pussy, Inc. Manufacturers and Distribu-tors Los Angeles California. Very spiritual huh?

Some people say that the *things* are eating them. It's really the trees they eat peo-ple at night vampires come out and dance on the graves of people who died before their time. Dogs start meowing and the pussies start barking.

I've seen those who walk around late nights with huge human heads attached to the bodies of lizards and snails bats and crows some say we need an exorcism here the straight citizens are scared.

Every time they discover the savior they kill him, this time with broken whisky bottles legs from broken chairs flower pots, anything. He does not become the savior till he's dead. They push him back into the *idea* of himself. What if he releases the idea of *Her*. Then what.

I deliberately selected defected lumber each piece was wrong but they all fitted into each other without nails. No friction.

The dream say she jumps out the window and nobody ever understands why. They eat out they eat in, they sleep in they sleep out. When he's in her he cannot understand. When she is outside herself she knows too much.

He drives the nail into the wood.

The boy cut the strips of wood with the automatic blade the strips like white flesh without blood dust settling on the eyelids. The buzz stays with me even weeks later while I'm reaching deep into the earth where some animal has died.

They went from the warehouse to the office, both places were cold. From the inside in the window boxes of nails metal strips catalogs hammers and wood glue for sale. It's cold.

After Christmas the super sale on thresholds: rose colored thresholds perky thresholds feminine thresholds snuggly thresholds creamy white blueberry blue strawberry rose thresholds ripe banana yellow and king-size thresholds!

The boy who wore a red shirt all the time was seduced by the . . .

The one who liked oranges died of innocence and ignorance.

That family that bottled goose grease was arrested.

"Those of you who have colds *must* go to the drugstore."

My plumber uses coffee grounds to unstop sinks he was arrested for this. In court he entered a plea of guilty though it was noted that fifty percent of the time his technique worked. Deep down in that hole who knows . . .

People driving home in cars alone have absolute privacy they can see others but . . .

They let him out of prison and he slept for days in a washroom beneath the sink where the smell of women was still strong.

The boy who lit three cigarettes from one match was struck dead by lightning. His remains are kept inside his mother's imagination where there is room for a whole civilization.

I went to see the guru. His eyes were weak but he could still sit still in his first and last judgments. The librarians with rubber breasts were there too.

44

The cigars old men smoke are going to be taken from them one of these days then the whole world will reach its turning point, the threshold will revolve.

There's a war going on so you see a lot of soldiers walking around without arms and real legs.

That girl I told you about still wears her mother's raspberry ribbon and sings in the shower of her abortions, dreams and . . .

Old people spend the day on the phone talking to other old people, there is connection, quiet, almost silent, underground connection . . .

A young girl, fed up, went to the supermarket naked and climbed into a Time Clock where the workers punch out.

Those husbands and fathers who do not carry their womenfolk across thresholds may be revolutionaries.

Saturday he went down to his car in the garage and found the engine ripped to pieces the hair of an animal was all over it.

The sun does not go deep into the ocean.

The skin torn at the edges of love heals very quickly.

Grown men dressed as women in high heels strut about in their tiny rooms trying to understand what happened . . .

"Too much honey turns sour in the fat stomach it is wise to give in to your fate may be fear of many so you fear many. Rats under the skin does not necessarily mean you having a nightmare."

Ludovic Janvier

From *Face*

so it's incapacious that we want to write . . . at least the semensea . . . a bit of the . . . sneering vampire on top of the numbed woman . . . great possessor but with the eyes . . . never slow to fly off into the easy bodies of fables where he indulges credulous in all his exploits . . . there the stunning erection . . . there the ocean's spasms . . . there dreadful sperm . . . but forbidden . . . and as if . . . forbidden facing bodies under sun . . . true bodies walking with long strides . . . there refused in advance . . . there prowls about his eye crafty as if starving parading in front of whores high-booted thighs nude up to the flower all of them men hesitant in cavalcade . . . and at the first warning where was he seen so long . . . but deployed on the cute one standing up warm proving in amazement . . . becoming tense at least toward a flash of piquant . . . a glance at the intimate mist . . . in order to come back from sugary fireworks rending right in the silk . . . exiles . . . secures . . . exiles . . . secures . . . exiles . . .

they could verify it on him hands and mouths greedy then patient then resigned while waiting for their choppers to give up . . . may faith come . . . and the little cad rise . . . waking he reels about hindered from homo into hetero . . . dreaming he seeks a beautiful object on which to graft himself champion . . . one night isn't he found at a contest of hands to groin . . . at an official masturbation with a jury of philes and manes attentively in concert . . . seated the nearest competitor extricates from the bulging linen an enormous . . . violet . . . formidable muscle . . . proof as ever . . . his flail hand can scarcely get around it . . . with a musician's gesture he lightly caresses the tumescence . . . a few seconds . . . one hears the summons the rumbling when the giant contracts . . . miraculous expulsion . . . gushes to the sky in a prodigious stream and then a translucent puddle . . . the scene stupefies then fades . . . let's not talk about another night without seeing him on his back under an assembly of crimsoned and evil members enormous in a circle swallowing with great gulps . . . this grail lasts a while then is forgotten . . . a long time in the same blackness a tall nude young brunette with movements slow as foliage swoons at the very instant when he is ready to melt in her . . . to diffuse there burning . . . this idol's long seasons . . . then presto vanishes like everything else . . . and that's why restricted diet mental feast he trots through the world like a true mongoloid of fuckery . . . not trots . . . floats rather . . . minuscule artaban under the swellings of gossip . . . hydrocephalic for images . . . glider big eye on faces searching the searched . . . on glances playing dirty . . . on the recruiting symphony of gestures . . . on legs lifted high . . . passing every festival lost . . . then punish sun and self . . . paid in the cinema wishing the deluge or eternal winter on himself living women living men . . . then frenzy . . . fury in his head flowing into shadow where at least there is a respite of untroubled seeing . . . then each time the same beating heart . . . blinded by the habitual blackness just as soon as the door is closed . . . the cavern . . . ah to be there . . . relax that's it . . . peace to the eye that searches between two heads for the jumble of lights the ink of darkness on the visible grain of the canvas . . . steeps there crystalline cornea iris . . . shakes off the wetness . . .

all the profiles in the hall are swept away at once by the light of the image . . . the screen is a white shore . . . all the profiles at once in the dark . . . the blackness of the sky at night . . . after having stood next to him her face lifted she moved back to a corner of the room her eyes sparkling in the semi-darkness the spot of her long white dress on the darkness of the partition the darkness of the wood the darkness of the railing showing up like lace on the only wall bathed by the moon before long discovered by the camera that revolved isn't it pretty . . . all around the croakings of toads . . . enormous ones no doubt with beating hearts visible within their throats . . . branches are bent by a racing in the wild ramshackle park . . . flow and ebb of the sea running against the sandbar . . . breaking into a frothy sibilant on the beach below . . . it is she . . . her lips full-fleshed . . . her eyes aquaslut . . . her head thrown back . . . it is she whom he'll see again when awakened he returns to his sun then to his shadow to his walls to his night he will seize himself stiff vibrant distended he will floculate a handful dazzled with images ah do we ever love the cinema . . . seeing her . . . someone sees her question in a rough voice the native servant coming back up from the beach his torso nude and wet . . . imagining her . . . someone imagines her leaning upon him drinking salt and water . . . the double hem of her lips together then apart then together greedy on the black supple shining skin imagined seen gluttonous female searching for the groin for the thick unsheathed stiff muscle to bite to lick to suck to swallow up eat me drink me bitch it's ava she's eating us yum her mouth around . . .

48

and you can believe that scarcely defended by a rampart of a similar shadow he is going to glide still seated the dreamer to the sea with words from another beach same thirst . . . there . . . the water rises . . . seethes . . . spreads out on tiles of foam its flabella . . . froths . . . goes down . . . is drunk . . . rises again . . . etc. . . . seen from behind she is walking there her feet bare her breasts high her uncovered legs shining with water her long thighs where her short dress stops splashed with spray . . . muscular ass in his hands pubis in his mouth taste of salt . . . her feet shake off sand at every step . . . no doubt at the bottom of each imprint is a bit of sea . . . seeing the rifle slowly aimed . . . seeing its long black scope lined up on top of the barrel . . . seeing the thick lens where four clear lines form the two diameters of a circle . . . seeing at their intersection a bull's-eye drawn in . . . it is the ideal center the point over there where the bullet should be imbedded . . . seeing rifle scope lens in our eyesight move up the length of the distant back divide it into four surfaces plus the fragile center reach the neck search for the nape find it bending deviating from the axis at every step lose it find it again in the fragile center in the bull's-eye drawn in look for the rhythm of the deviations lose it find it again center more exactly on the delicate area seeing there the tanned skin of the neck below the short hair . . . the bullet would puncture the epidermis shatter the vertebra medulla cerebellum gush into the mouth immediately filled with blood . . . the woman walking not knowing near the water exposed . . . not firing or is he going to tear the sade to bits for us . . . the camera leaves her . . . there is the sound as if in a dream . . . the camera recaptures her . . . seeing her fall she falls seeing her fall to her knees rolling slowly on

the sand to her side . . . immobilized . . . she is immobilized . . . the water sparkles . . . it rises to her mouth . . . it beats on her dress plastered to her breasts her
crotch her thighs . . . it falls back carries off a little blood . . . the following
wave . . . spit your blood spit . . . the following wave pushes aside a high fringe of
foam . . . stretches out as it rises . . . froth . . . comes up to beat against the
darkened dress . . . sparkles in the sun . . . enters the open mouth falls back rose-
ate goes back the length of the saturated sand . . . a little blood mingles with the
last bubbles with the pellicle of water that glided toward the next lapping wave
scintillating all along its fringe of foam . . . dead eyes closed now nude drowned
by the green water the length of the body lying on its right side . . . empties the
mouth . . . washes the smile upon the teeth . . . disturbs as it rises the long dark
hair on her head the rich pubic hair smooths them as it falls back glides to the
sea . . . ah the cinema . . .

yes the best ambush is total emulsion . . . ambuscade for worlds for bodies that
one eyesupon . . . well sheltered in woodland framing artaban for example is re-
discovering forgotten grass . . . the tall half-sun half-shade with long hollows under the wind . . . flexible stems leaves umbels nettles shaken slow and return to
their flight on foot . . . trampled by boots among . . . they crush . . . the pursu-
ing . . . one myopics tiny green spiders . . . daddy longlegs spread apart bending
stem after stem . . . ants under clover still lower . . . among them trampled by
bare legs entwined with plants . . . the pursued . . . among them at the edge of
the woods flight of skirts that rise corollas float in slow motion fall . . . among
them leaning in the penumbra lighted from below the face of a child searching in
the coolness . . . coming from a distance approaching unpunished traveling . . .
dulling to the same level the lightness of organdies linens tulles in which backward there beat long legs thighs in full foam . . . backward on the meadow showing at the edge of the stream with white pebbles showing with little cries showing oh bitch in the lights of the shadow . . . washed away by the eye the least
visible woman . . . as if . . . washed away by words toward sweetness . . . fleece
. . . satin . . . the mute brunette stretched out mouth shaping a yes . . . pale with
freckles . . . the black woman polishes our tongue level with her rosy night
. . . what false vision for the voracious . . . what false vision in cinemaseas where

a look rises washed . . . it was the beach polished to dead . . . it will be the bursting storms on silks linens plastered heavily to the breasts the long legs of innumerable . . . their faces damp . . . their lips blood on their uncovered teeth . . . eye to their eye immense bath full image . . . their look entirely on the look of the man bent over in the shadows who cinemadrinks . . . their eyes on the eyes of the green water in the whiteness then a wink . . . on the brown coffee in the immense whiteness of milk then a wink . . . on blue the blue water of eyes washed with tears in the rosy blood then a wink . . . who comes to us so it is the tall woman with the smile of regret she stops eternal at the edge of the eye . . . black ink . . . fully lighted she is the one who comes to you in her muslins her silk smiling under her big summer hat that shadows her mouth with sadness . . . she stops at the edge of the eye . . . black ink . . . fully lighted she sets out again from the depths comes to him one thigh one leg slowly after the other lifting the muslins the silks smiling . . . she stops at the edge of the eye . . . sets out again from the depths comes nude toward his gaze with slow strides . . . heavy her breasts at each step swaying mammaries . . . from which sucks the lapping dreamer . . . sucks . . . hides against them mouth and regrets . . . raises and again raises his eyes to the smile of the mist black hair undone wan smile long blond locks the double pulp over the teeth of the woman stopping at the edge of the eye . . . although from the back one dashes forth delicate under the rain . . . slender from the back beset by the rain mingled with the others . . . although she steps through the gusts of wind . . . moves off wet from the storm . . . nude light tongue at her ass yes if her butt swept by the storm is streaming a crack then tongue can whip around inside its full . . . yes if your butt caught in gusts by the storm in large hot drops and if streaming a crack spreads out violet eyelet in which to probe as much as you want drink lick lap slurp swig hurrah for the cinema . . .

and that's the way he staggers about head first trusting in these maelstroms of shadows and lights . . . plunges loyal into the spiders' caves . . . into the bloody subterranean passages . . . comes back up howling to the river banks . . . scaling dizzily the tower or the belfry where the grinning monster is going to swing in the sky ah . . . gulps down catastrophes sated . . . sees and again sees bodies atrocious under torture bleeding lost . . . simpleton drinks without thirst ready for every squall . . . barely does he wink the sucker to see himself seen . . . searching for memory . . . clinging to the time prior to the abyss that there they are all carried off at top speed the chair and the man downstream away from this rain of bullets . . . the thousand crystals of the image bombard the fibrillae . . . shaking the humors . . . gelatin and its bromides all burst into stories . . . then he slips by smug in the cavern of glories . . . blinds himself to the shaking fabulous shocks of the emulsion upon the screen . . . wallowed in the procession down there isn't he wasting his life the devourer . . . when he gets up from his seat he is anesthetized . . . ambling away from bodies . . . looks . . . aspects . . . crossing sun like night because for others the summer of the eyes . . . we prefer pregnant stiff to convey even to sleep and its slow images . . . to convey as a schoolboy still . . . in perpetual terror . . . to convey the last gestures seen and again seen the looks the aspects the voices all renounced in sadness once the confusion if successful . . .

oh shit always to see oneself seen . . . to write oneself written . . .

    —trans. William H. Matheson and Emma Kafalenos

Disorder

Open sores w/ faces mug on tv specials
calld reality calld up in dere calld
whatchacallum whatchacallit, whatitis calld
stand in line waste yr life in line death crying
streets smash line drive cars by zooming we live under
a heavy pall a tarpaulin of struggle tears struggle momentary
splendid laughter working people struggling for reality, the beat of the times

is it out there
the question answered too many times
without being put into practice

put out there by dawn smudging its drunks
its faggot preachers shoving crucifixes up in em to come before the sun does
too many times, amidst the books in rockefellers memorial library a time bomb
just now the assembly man rises
trudges into the bathroom

the lines of fire stand in silhouette in pre-bird purity
the scrapple from the apple is the people resisting the fifty cent fare
& some keepin teachers out of the schools for talking trick shit about education
a comrade mad weaving along the railroad tracks screaming she hates all
    communists

it is the hour of conflict, antagonism, struggle
the world turning autumn in warpaint
everything silently
prepares to scream

Das Kapital

Strangling women in the suburban bush
they bodies laid around rotting while martinis are drunk
the commuters looking for their new yorkers feel a draft
& can get drunker watching the teevee later on the Ford
replay. There will be streams of them coming, getting off
near where the girls got killed. Two of them strangled by
the maniac.
There are maniacs hidden everywhere cant you see? By the dozens
and double dozens, maniacs by the carload (tho they *are*
a minority). But they terrorize us uniformly, all over the place
we look at the walls of our houses, the garbage cans parked full
strewn around our defaulting cities, and we cd get scared. A rat
eases past us on his way to a banquet, can you hear the cheers raised
through the walls, full of rat humor. Blasts of fire, some woman's son will
    stumble
and die with a pool of blood around his head. But it won't be the maniac. These
    old houses
crumble, the unemployed stumble by us straining, ashy fingered, harassed. The
    air is cold
winter heaps above us consolidating itself in degrees. We need a aspirin or
    something, and
pull our jackets close. The baldhead man on the television set goes on in a
    wooden way
his unappetizing ignorance cannot be stood, or understood. The people turn the
    channel
looking for Good Times and get a negro with a pulldown hat. Flashes of maniac
    shadows before

bed, before you pull down the shade you can see the leaves being blown down
    the street
too dark now to see the writing on them, the dates, and amounts we owe. The
    streets too
will soon be empty, after the church goers go on home having been saved again
    from the
Maniac . . . except a closeup of the chief mystic's face rolling down to his hands
    will send
shivers through you, looking for traces of the maniacs life. Even there among
    the mythophrenics.

What can you do? It's time finally to go to bed. The shadows close around you
    and the room is still.
Most of us know there's a maniac loose. Our lives a jumble of frustrations and
    unfilled
capacities. The dead girls, the rats noise, the flashing somber lights, the dead
    voice on
television, was that blood and hair beneath the preacher's fingernails? A few
    other clues

we mull them over as we go to sleep, the skeletons of dollar bills, traces of dead
    used up
labor, lead away from the death scene until we remember a quiet fit that
    everywhere
is the death scene. Tomorrow you got to hit it sighs through us like the wind,
    we got to
hit it, like an old song at radio city, working for the yanqui dollarrrrr, when we
    were
children, and then we used to think it was not the wind, but the maniac
    scratching against
our windows. Who is the maniac, and why everywhere at the same time . . .

Street Reflection

In a sunset bourgeois world, leaves flicker like evening always
even in the middle of the day
talking to young comrades, about the new day beyond this
laying out the correct line, and back to hear/here, green window direction
child noise direction, converged, television dry scatting, the yells the yells
amidst the searching for firm theoretical base for it all (supersonic swift steel
piercing a space) speeding untouched between the blind vampires of the "left"
    and
the more dangerous terrifying stuffed & bloody vampires of the right.

Sometimes the way it all is becomes "very acute"
                                        means
                            right tight up
                    "empty headed poseurs" bumping into . . .
            Empty Headed?? Is that naivete?? Clar-
            ence Kelly in Washington, half drunk after lunch
                trying to put together a slick way to take us out, and
            we want to see the dick tracy badge before we bust the bucktooth
        baby mensheviks as the same kind of killers as their spiritual
    leader, "Nelson The Knife"?
                            Either get hip or get lost, is the slogan of
                            the moment.

6

The Fragmentation of Identity and Perspective

For Amiri Baraka, as for few avant-garde writers today, the mystery can be penetrated. The confusions—the shadows, the flickers that obscure vision—are necessary effects of the ideological world we inhabit. They prevent clear perception, a "correct line" and a theoretical basis for action. Only with the tool of Marxist analysis, Baraka states, can the origins and limits of such obscurity be determined. It is upon such an analysis that any artist interested in significant change must base his or her creations; otherwise, the avant-garde can only remain the unfocused and diversionary complaints of alienated individuals. His is the belief that politics can directly inform art, and the knowledge that to inquire of the avant-garde is to confront the sociological role of art in this culture.

His faith, however, is not shared by the many contemporary avant-garde writers who sustain the avant-garde tradition's strong tendency to be sympathetic to Marxism, but who ultimately reveal an anarchistic and "non-ideological" bias. Addressed to no specific class, yet shaped by the immediate context of bourgeois culture and its audience, this avant-garde emphasizes the immediacy and the drama of isolated individuals' struggles to come to terms with the negative forces that govern their lives. The avant-garde's belief in the efficacy of this process, even without a clear vision of what the new knowledge will permit or demand, generates its constant stylistic experimentation and, occasionally, its social antagonism. Yet it is now an art of criticism, with no message other than the need for continuous questioning. It is an art of unrest, with no clearly defined audience other than those predisposed to doubt and to search.

In this avant-garde, then, a constant questioning is taking place, a mystery is confronted. A mystery? Well, perhaps only a confusion. The patterns of approach and withdrawal, of questioning and avoidance, are so persistent as to be almost ritualized. Yes, an attempt is being made, an attempt to connect with the reality of our lives—lives seemingly built of fragments in an environment not worthy of our trust. As often as not, the attempt is aborted even before it is fully articulated. Reading contemporary avant-garde texts can be a frustrating experience, for although the works seek a total vision, they distrust that vision and themselves once it is approached. An awareness of social fragmentation mitigates against a unified aesthetic or political vision, but simultaneously, the suspicion of the restrictive and deceptive complacency of the reigning social order leads the avant-garde toward an affirmation of the potentially liberating spirit of willed fragmentation. Consequently, the works disrupt all messages of presumed authority, ultimately even their own. Because they rebel against social totalization and cultural homogenization, they appear to fall back not into vital individualism, but into dispersive fragmentation.

Nevertheless, discord and denial are declared to be the primary agents of a critical spirit. And if the avant-garde remains an art of liberation today, it is principally one that champions the primacy of doubt, disruption, and self-criticism. But the sense of confusion remains strong. The self-reflexive process of questioning oneself and one's environment prevents a clear perspective or a stable framework of judgment. The very existence of such a framework is denied by many avant-garde writers. Consequently, every insight gained is itself subject to doubt. And how can one express in fragments anything other than fragmentation?

Friederike Mayröcker's fragmentary narratives and fitful dialogues present pained efforts to describe experiences, express emotions, or embrace fleeting ideals, all of which elude articulation. Everything seems unstable, including the speaking voices. Characters talk at cross purposes. Metaphors and the situations they would illuminate are held in tenuous balance. Abstractions separate from lived experience and become independent artifices, enticing in their presumed significance, yet unfulfilling in their distance from human reality. The characters long for some degree of fixity, some stability that was once promised in a past ideal or image but that is now recognized as only a fiction. Those fictions of meaning, of beauty, of personal closeness or individual assurance haunt the present dominated by a sense of decay and fragmentation. Every attempt to project a new ideal, to break "out of reality," is doomed to become only the basis of some future nostalgia or moment of disillusion. Above all, now and in the future, the characters will fall out of the dream of the ideal into the realization of their essential vulnerability to time and loss.

Toby Lurie writes "conversation poems" in which two independent yet entwining voices reflect and extend each other's message. Yet in "I People" their supportive themes concern mutual exclusion, the separation of individuals from themselves and from each other. One can read each verse separately, but the poem's parallel structure merges the separate voices in a polyphony of alienation.

Marvin Cohen's texts are monologues of a mind trying to fix itself and experience in speech, to give voice to experience and time which it realizes cannot be mastered by its available tools—consciousness and language. The message, echoed in so many contemporary self-reflexive fictions, could result in a state of impotence and desperation. This mind divided against itself realizes that to know is to diminish or falsify its subject, including itself. To think is to be out of step with experience; the artifice of thought finds itself ever dependent on the unknown which gives it birth but which it will betray. But the voice which animates these self-conscious and amused texts delights in its fictiveness, making itself a self-conscious artifice in which the mind's persona achieves a degree of abstraction that makes it read like an essay. It announces its temporarily independent status as an indirect form of life, usurping the stage until the physical and the unknown once again upset the metaphysical and the articulated.

Scott Helmes's text expresses itself through another form of extreme abstraction—an equation in which the known fragments of experience, our relationships, suffering, pleasures, and awareness of time, are balanced by unknown factors and powers which exist independently of us. Unfortunately, it is only too apparent that the X factor, the unknown by which the equation will be completed, will not be discovered until the answer is provided by experience, thus rendering the equation ultimately irrelevant.

Friederike Mayröcker

Narrating of a Narration

red, he said, red and as hard as chalk.

chalk is not hard, she said.

red, he said, and as hard as chalk, and producible from everything, he said.

from everyone, she said, by everyone producible, poetry must be producible by everyone.

from everything, he said.

revolution poetry, she said.

no, he said, no.

reality based on values, she said, contemplation.

new contemplation perhaps, he said.

a hand, he said, with a baker's tong reaching from the shop into a chock-full confectionery window, removing a segment from an already cut pie, and you in front of the window, he said.

a comparison, she said, questioningly.

intellectual compulsion toward truth, he said, intentions under strain.

like pallas athene sprung fully equipped from the head of zeus, she said questioningly.

and before the shop door a mat for the dog, he said.

a bit higher a hook to hang the leash, he said, above that an enameled sign WE CANNOT ENTER and beneath it the head of a dog, he said.

you must break out, she said, *out of reality*, but break it down with you, down into the abyss as you fall.

and how did that become you, he said.

from next door, she said, I heard in the morning silence the curtains being drawn back from the windows.

some localities, he said, leave me with pleasant, others with unpleasant feelings and thoughts, he said.

paths, streets, entranceways, vistas, squares, lawns, passages, buildings, wall angles, gardens, he said, without my knowing why.

such reflections are not new to me, she said.

but what have I done wrong, why has it all gone wrong, I did all that I could to make it work.

we know much too little of each other, he said.

and then, she said, I tried out my left eye to see how it functioned.

meanwhile we were walking down a side street that ran along the highway, a short stretch always back and forth as if we were waiting for someone who at any moment should come out of the house, standing without neighborhood here at the wayside, and I stared a long time into the lemon-yellow sky.

in a cold bedroom, he said, when I climb into a cold bed, slip undressed under the white wool blanket, I can tell, he said, how my bed gradually grows warm with the warmth of my body.

with the person I was at ten, he said, I have nothing more in common.

—trans. Harriett Watts

With Each Clouded Peak

what a conflict, he said.
until it's finally to the point that.
after all, one would like to make something substantial of it.
it's a question of maintaining a fiction, she said.
a balancing act.
of slapping, he said, of slapping beauty in the face.
so he sat on the higher pipes, in the higher garden a light was burning.
in the higher garden, he said, the sister cities.
and in bitter march, she said, in bitterest spring.
in the higher court, he said, elsewhere.
still in bitter march, he said, the heaved-up stratification in glass.
curtains of ice, he said, bound back with cord.
the sweep of the drapes immense, the miracle profane, he said.
like peacock splendor.
in a, pianos, temples she said, she laughed.
and a millstone about the neck of Saint Florian, he said, he laughed.
the fiction, namely, that one has an important office to carry out.
the problem is to maintain the fiction, she said.
likewise to slap beauty in the face, he said.
an image, after all, that is often strained.
a celestial parenthesis, a sustaining angel, he said.
sustaining angel, stark blue, toppled from early winter's blind
horizon, he said, down on me, on my startled skull pate.
storms down on us, in early winter out of a blind sky, splashing plaster on our
skull pate, diter rot.

and onward, piano-thunder, water stream, with stark blue demands.
aesthetic, ethical demands, he said.
reading finger, wordmaker, sheep lice in the meadow's brown pelt, he said.
water-cheap, fallen number.
millstone about the neck of Saint Florian, he said.
with each clouded peak.
she had such a lost smile, he said.
as she followed us out of the hospital room into the corridor to see us to the gate.
saying something about a fallen number.

we didn't know what it could mean.
then she stood on the porch and waved after us, before she turned away, turned back, went back.
poor, happy child, he said.
in the higher garden, he said, the sister cities.
from things to come, he said, the ships return.
so that we can feel what we shall feel, when we, a few years older, think back on the time in which we now live, he said.
so that we can think what we shall think at that future time, when we'll look back on a time in which we were younger than we'll be then; a kind of self-envy.
still in bitter march, she said.
the star fields.
time-downward on their way.
whereupon anastas sank his teeth into a drinking glass, he said.
and busheled ears through the district.
an electric formula, he said.
that is to say, as the hours passed like minutes, the minutes like seconds, those again like days, the days again like years, those again like hours, the hours like minutes, and those like seconds and those again like days and those again like years, like decades.
and those again, he said.
stared into the screen of my time displacement.
nights at the window, she said, when looking out I leaned downward.
and the beads hanging down to my earlobes, she said.

a sketch, he said, a view, namely, over the landscape.
a view, expanding tributary, reflecting little towns, noisy.
incorporated casually into the book, he said.
until we, because of the rain, he said.
acquire verdigris, he said.
glistening and green in the forehills, she said, and again and again the longing,
she said.
to attach ourselves to things, places, landscapes, to search them out again.
the old granaries in the village, wildly overgrown international way-stations, a
camping site.
old iron, crumbling grave statuary, stumps of pillars.
proliferating green, a path.
above it a shimmer, she said, sighted in earliest childhood.
as soon as we, hesitant, step by step, had entered the sunny inner courtyard of the
farm house, marveling happily.
electric horizon, meadows rust, he said.
farmland, farm wagon.
toddling alongside, he said, sunk in introspective melancholy, scratching words
down on bits of paper.
which we later mislaid, lost.
trembling sudden love, then, he said.
bewitching, seemingly invincible, obscuring everything for years.
from things to come, he said, world-traveled flower seed.
bell script, of things to come.
a flying fortress, he said.
and then falling out of line again, he said, nothing but falling out of line and
alarming friends.

    —trans. Harriett Watts

65

In a Run-Down Neighborhood

a storm of images, he said, like a storm they come and with everything time so short, he said, and still I would have thought I could eventually win him over to our side.

back then, he said, when we all went out to eat fish together and I helped her out of the car she answered as she planted first her right foot and then immediately her left foot and lowered her head so as not to hit the car, why not, why not, maybe some day you can win him over to your ideas, he said, but then time proved to be so short, he said.

a raw world, he said, coming out of a raw world into a smooth one, and time so short, her letter, he said, was old fashioned, written in an ornate hand, but the cadences rang true and space between the lines, like the breathing of someone quite agitated and then, he said, we all drove together to New Orleans and I think he enjoyed the old city where the French were once in power and later in a run-down neighborhood, he said, the black jazz musicians.

I'm looking forward to your presence, he said, it will be springtime.

a rose, he said, today I have a rose on my windowsill.

nor do I have much time left, he said.

a rose, he said, today I have a rose on my windowsill, he said, my wife picked it for me this morning, so roses bloom here in December as well, he said.

I hope, he said, you will have a chance to meet your translator here, he said, a young banker.

I know exactly what he'll say then, he said, for once not to follow all these damned signs, he will say, reality is damned attractive, he will say, reality.

as we, he said, were leaving the Hotel Callas in Cologne beuys stood somewhat elevated in the gateway, he said, with arms spread wide, thin white face, surrounded by young people, spoke, was questioned, answered and it rained heavily and because of the strong gusty winds many had closed their umbrellas, he said, because of the wind.

in a run-down neighborhood, he said, and as beuys waved his arms up and down.

it was raining heavily, he said, she called us up one night, even though she lived directly beneath us and could have just as easily come up the few steps and as she suddenly telephoned us upstairs, he said, we shouldn't be making such a racket upstairs, he said, because they all couldn't sleep, he said, we would have to do something about it.

and it is also precisely this split second, he said, of exposure, of being exposed perhaps, he said, this dionysiac rush, he said, this dirty mutation, he said, that awaits us all when the green expanse of leaves is broken by white dots, spots and stripes, he said, it will be a lovely time of the year and I'm looking forward to your presence, it will be spring a lovely time of the year.

the alpine republics, he said, where the French were once in power and later in a run-down neighborhood black jazz musicians.

give it with only half a gesture, he said, in order to inspire reassurance in the others, he said, letting friendly waters freeze over, on the phone, he said, she told me that she cared as much as ever, but that she couldn't stand my presence at the moment, a few weeks should pass, we should let a few weeks go by.

we have to take things as they come, he said, the fact that time is so short, he said.

the effort, he said, we spend in order to maintain the substance, he said.

how futile, she wore a pink swim cap, stood in the midst of a shoe-store display and asked—to take out?

yes, he said, better to suffer injustice than to commit it and in the end one is marked by what one has done, snake people, wolf people, sirens, she wore a pink swim cap, he said, a misunderstanding on his part, he said, that's how things are.

from the hand of the confectioner, he said, the tin shears, places, he said, placelessness, he said, placelessness grasping, one winter morning with almost no morning light.

what torments us, he said, what strikes us, moves us, today on my windowsill.

roses bloom here in December as well, in a run-down neighborhood, on my windowsill today I have a rose picked for me by my wife, so roses bloom in December as well in a run-down neighborhood, nor do I have much time left, he said, I haven't much time either.

—trans. Harriett Watts

Toby Lurie

I People

1) I   I have   I have become
2)   People   people touch   people touch and drift

1) I have become the dream.
2)   People touch and drift apart.

1) My mind   has released me
2)   in their intricate cells   floating

1) from reality.   I   I am wind
2)   lockt in.   And touching

1)   I am wind and fog
2) and touching becomes   and touching becomes memory

1) floating   floating in the dream
2)   yearning   yearning for renewal

1) which   which I   which I have become.
2)   people   people touch

1)   The center   the center has shifted
2) people touch again   drift apart

1)   balance   an abstraction
2) drift apart abandoned to ambitions   touching

1)   my mouth
2) touching becomes   becomes an unanswered pain

1) my mouth is open   but offers
2)   people touch   word upon word

1) but offers no sound   my tears   my tears smell strangely
2)   flesh   flesh

1)   I am   I am the star
2) flesh upon flesh   and drift   and drift apart

1) in an absurd drama   it is comedy
2)   crying to be rescued

1)   the laughter   is tearing
2) as the ceremony   of touching

1)   is tearing at my heart
2) of touching and drifting   repeats itself

1) as I drift   as I drift through the dream   which I
2)   again   again

1)   which I have become.
2) again   again.

Marvin Cohen

Outbursts and Norms

The unknown came racing out of me. As it became known, it returned back inside, more slowly, in its newly transformed form of "known." Then I slowed down. A lengthy lull set in, between excitement peaks. I wore dull knowledge. Ignorance was frozen into dormancy. When would it break out, again?

71

An Untamed Interiority, That Turns Down All Institutional Circumscribing and Resists the Name Plates for the Systematically Defined, as the World Can't Swallow It Down.

Clogged with food, rippling on the swell of anxiety, undulating with the roar of drink, bitter with hope, lyrical with terror, paralyzed by memory, lurching between unknowns, I became suddenly blind with love.

The cluttered instant can't recognize itself. It's packed with a squabble of contradictions. Its rippling interiority is all unrelieved discord. It's a resisting wilderness to our civilized principle of consistency, and offers no neck to the collar of domestication. It sprawls unstill, and keeps no steady figure for the branding measure to chart into the known. But it has its own felt existence, however unprocessed to worldly terms outside, where instants are immediately parceled off to the historical.

It's been living. Let its chaos go undisturbed. It's forgone itself, when understood.

Thought Is Out of Step with Life, in Their Crooked Dance

We can never live what we think at the time we think it, nor think what we live at the time we live it. Consciousness is always just too late. Once we catch up with it, it's already been altered by memory. We fall behind in consciousness whatever has provoked that consciousness. Intellectual processes weave their analytical webs in the vacant wall angles of our time gaps between what has happened and our attempts to recover it. We're never quite there in thought, we're never a direct witness, at our own events. They pass us by. Our intellect must dine on the remnant glow of their echoes, not on their instantaneousness itself. By means of thought, we're ever living indirectly. Or rather, by our living indirectly, we're made to think. Or rather, our thought *is* our indirect living. Reflection is after the event, not during; *about* the event, once the event has stopped being that phase of process just undergone. We're never on time. Consciousness steps in the gap. In essence, it's a time-obsession. There's that relentless urgency, to somehow catch up. We're always late. This is emotionalized, by pathos, in poignance. We have no identities: for there's no identity of what happens to us with our consciousness of it. Thought is always at work, compensating for this. But thought is *about* life. Life eludes it, being lived.

Three Outbursts of Time

1. AUTOBIOGRAPHY STRIPPED OF FACTS

I used to have intense philosophical moments. They became physical, which enriched the philosophy. Then they became too physical, and the philosophy stopped. The physical stopped. Then they both started again together. They bunched into inside-outside substance, with the fissure of a mental vacuum in between: the core of nothingness. I'm trying to fill that core, but fail.

2. TIME IN DISCONNECTED CONSCIOUSNESS

My life is turning into its opposite. Here I am, thinking about it. The world and I combine into thought. I'm leaving the world. Then I leave thought too. That gives me pause. I want to slow down. I'd like to have a thought, and stay that way.

But if I "stay" that way, I'll be suffering. So I'll move on, to change the suffering, and find some pleasant feelings at odd moments. Consciousness is a risk. Lots of pain, but some pleasure too. Truth is a consequence of the moment. It soon outdates itself, made obsolete by the succeeding moment. To arrest these changes, I try generalizing. But time is insulted by my generalizations, since the pseudo phoniness of time is a mental "eternity." So I move along, from me to me to me. Memory unifies the me's, to some degree.

3. MY SOLUTION

Time is happening to my thinking. But I ignore it, and go on thinking.

Scott Helmes

Non-Denominational

$$\frac{\text{Non-denominational}}{\text{coming accepted}} = \text{unknown/power}$$

you

$$\sum_{\text{me}} \times \text{infinity} \frac{\text{time}}{\text{tick}} = \frac{\text{second}}{\text{chance}} + \frac{\text{minute}}{\text{our}}$$

$$\frac{\text{pleasure/lost}}{+ \text{ pus } + \text{ pain}} = \frac{\text{suffering}}{\text{immensely}} \text{ aided} \quad + \quad \text{some}$$

$$\frac{\text{unknown quantity mixed} + \text{known factors}}{X}$$

$$\text{gives } \frac{\text{one}}{\text{one}} \text{ integration/} \frac{\text{times}}{\text{eternal}} \text{ unknown?}$$

which leaves one unanswered.

7

Restriction and Freedom: The Self in the Text

Feelings of restriction and freedom: an acceptance of the limits of self and the adventure of self-creation—these are the patterns of contemporary creation. Our participation in the forming of our world and the responsibility for asserting or rejecting meaning—these are the positive dimensions of the avant-garde impulse. But every text and fragmentary self also carries with it the knowledge of its inability to sustain itself, and every self-conscious being acknowledges an external power greater than itself.

The avant-garde response, peculiar to our time, is to turn these questions of perception and interpretation of the world back upon the creative process, in order to locate in the primary act of creation the complexities of self-definition and articulation. It is to determine how much the individual is already shaped by his or her language and by the cultural values inherent in our discourse. Social reality is translated into patterns of cultural and ideological discourse, and personal knowledge is declared to be a function of individual positioning within inherited language.

For example, Raymond Federman's dense and deeply disturbing story, "The Voice in the Closet," is a record of the interaction of a writer and his language, and through that language, his subject—his horrifying past as a child who narrowly escaped the Holocaust and who, out of that experience, had to create a new self which ultimately became the writer of the story. Yet the past is neither easily revealed nor regarded. This text, Federman's "Season in Hell," bears witness to a number of interior tensions: the resistance of the present self to speak the brutal truth which was the basis of his previous writings, but which had been consciously transformed into fiction, and the tendency inherent in language itself to make of any articulated experience a fictive construct, hence to deflect the truth from direct vision. If, furthermore, all autobiography is fictive to the extent that language and the writer construct a persona, even while claiming to speak the truth, this story is even more painfully convoluted because it is about the forced creation of a new identity after the old one has been swept away by historical circumstances. That new and fictive identity is the basis of the persona telling the story and seeking a truth that would deny its very foundation. Federman, the persona and writer in his closed room, finds his creator in the child within the closet. Between the moments of origin and telling lies a history of mediations, of lived fictions and a series of poems and novels (*Among the Beasts*, *Double or Nothing*, *Take It or Leave It*) which necessarily, and to some extent conveniently, obscured the original reality which lay on the other side of the door and beyond articulation. Yet paradoxically, in the only voice available to it—the voice of fiction—that reality, the silence and the truth, demand in this text to be told and accuse the writer of avoiding the truth. Encoded in language and the closet, protected yet confined, the child, the writer, and the text encounter the limits and possibilities of their beginnings and self-presence. Text and creator, past and present, history and fiction confront and judge each other, only to reveal how much they define and undermine their respective beings.

Raymond Federman

The Voice in the Closet

here now again selectricstud makes me speak with its balls all balls foutaise sam says in his closet upstairs but this time it's going to be serious no more masturbating on the third floor escaping into the trees no the trees were cut down liar it's winter now delays no more false starts yesterday a rock flew through the windowpane voices and all I see him from the corner of my eye no more playing dumb boys in the street laughing up and down the pages en fourire goofing my life it's a sign almost hit him in the face scared the hell out of him as he waits for me to unfold upstairs perhaps the signal of a departure in my own voice at last a beginning after so many detours relentless false justifications in the margins more to come in my own words now that I may speak say I the real story from the other side extricated from inside roles reversed without further delay they pushed me into the closet on the third floor I am speaking of us into a box beat me black and blue question of perspective how it should have started in my little boy underwear I'm speaking of me sssh it's summertime lies again we must hide the boy sssh mother whispering in her tears hurts to lose all the time in the courtyard bird blowing his brains out on

alto guts squeaking lover man can you hear it now yellow feather cam
sent it to me at his fingertips plagiarizing my life boys passing in
the street they threw sand in his eyes it begins downstairs soldiers
calling our names his too federman all wrong don't let him escape no
not this time must save the boy full circle from his fingers into my
voice back to him on the machine just heard the first tioli echo how
idiotic what did he expect callow it says after twenty years banging
his head against the wall rattling the old stories ah what's the use
watch him search in his dictionary callow unfledged youth almost hit
him in the face federman featherless little boy dammit in our closet
after so many false names foisted upon me evading the truth he wrote
all the doors opened to stare at my nakedness a metaphor I suppose a
twisted laugh wrong again writing himself into a corner inside where
they kept old newspapers delirious strokes of typographiphobia fatal
however only on occasions his fingers on the machine make me book of
flights speak traps evasions question of patience determination take
it or leave it of all places hundred years of solitary work down the
drain through the windowpane something about the futility of telling

experimenting with the peripatetic search for love self sex or is it
real people america aside from what is said there is nothing silence
sam again what takes place in the closet is not said irrelevant here
if it were to be known one would know it my life began in a closet a
symbolic rebirth in retrospect as he shoves me in his stories whines
his radical laughter up and down pulverized pages with his balls mad
fizzling punctuation question of changing one's perspective view the
self from the inside from the point of view of its capacity its will
power federman achieve the vocation of your name beyond all forms of
anthropologism a positive child anthropomorphism rather than the sad
off-spring of a family giggling they pushed me into the closet among
empty skins dusty hats my mother my father yes the soldiers they cut
little boys' hands old wife's tale send him into his life cut me now
from your voice not that I be what I was machines but what I will be
mother father quick downstairs already the boots same old problem he
tried oh how he tried of course imagining that the self must be made
remade caught from some retroactive present apprehended reinstated I
presume looking back how naive into the past my life began not again

whereas in fear my mother was crying softly as the door closes on me

I'm beginning to see my shape only from the past from the reverse of

farness looking to the present can one possibly into the future even

create the true me invent you federman with your noodles gambling my

life away double or nothing in your verbal delirium don't let anyone

interfere with our project cancel our journey in my own words inside

the real story again my father too coughing his tuberculosis as they

locked him into the boxcar they cut little boys' hands alone waiting

on his third floor crapping me on his paper what a joke the soldiers

quick sssh and all the doors slammed shut the boots in the staircase

where it should have started but not him no instead cunningly shoves

the statue of liberty at us very symbolic over the girl's shoulder I

tremble in his lies nothing he says about the past but I see it from

the corner of my eye even tried to protest while the outside goes in

then smiles among the beasts and writes one morning a bird flew into

my head ah what insolence what about the yellow star on my chest yes

what about it namredef the truth to say where they kept old wrinkled

clothes empty skins dusty hats and behind the newspapers stolen bags of sugar cubes how I crouched like a sphinx falling for his wordshit moinous but where were you tell me dancing when it all started where namredef when the door closed on me shouting I ask you when I needed you the most letting me be erased in the dark at random in his words scattered nakedly telling me where to go how many times yes how many times must he foist his old voice on me his detours cancellations ah that's a good one lies lies me to tell now procrastinations I warned him deep into my designs refusing to say millions of words wasted to say the same old thing mere competence never getting it straight his repetitions what really happened ways to cancel my life digressively each space relating to nothing other than itself me inside his hands progress quickly discouraged saying that it was mad laughter to pass the time two boxes correspondence of space the right aggregate while he inflicts false names on me distorts our beginning but now I stoop on the newspapers groping to the walls for the dimensions of my body while he stares at his selectricstud humping paper each space within itself becoming the figure of our unreality scratched from words the designs twirl just enough for me to speak and I fall for his crap to

become puppet believing he is me or vice versa born voiceless I wait
in the dark now down the staircase with their bundles moaning yellow
stars to the furnace the boots my mother father sisters too to their
final solution when I needed him the most last image of my beginning
to the trains to be remade unmade to shade the light and he calls me
boris when I stood on the threshold boris my first false name but he
erased that too in a stroke of impatience made me anonymous nameless
choose for yourself he mutters a name among infinite possibilities I
tried to protest gives us blank spaces instead while he hides inside
his own decomposition homme de plume hombre della pluma reverses his
real name namredef between the lines in the corners featherman sings
his signs anticipating his vocation leaps over the precipice cancels
the real story with exaggerations I watched him long ago make images
among the beasts how many false starts for me to go but where if the
door had opened by mid-afternoon the world would be alive dust burnt
pains in the guts squeaking pretending to be dead I replay the scene
down the staircase perhaps I slept the whole time and a bird flew in
my head past his face through the windowpane scared him face to face

with oldman I threw sand in his eyes struck his back with a stick in his delirium whining like a wounded animal I squat on the newspapers unfolded here by shame to defecate my fear as he continues to scream multiplying voices within voices to silence me holding my penis away not to piss on my legs clumsily continues to fabricate his design in circles doodles me up and down his pages of insolence two closets on the third floor separate correspondence of birth in time seeking the right connection meaning of all meanings but from this angle never a primary phenomenon to end again reducible to nonsense excrement of a beginning in the dark I folded the paper into a neat package for the birds smelling my hands by reflex or to disintegrate years later but he ignores that too obsessed by fake images while sucking his pieces of stolen sugar on the roof by the ladder outside the glass door the moon tiptoed across the clouds curiosity drove me down the staircase but I stumbled on the twelfth step and fell and all the doors opened dumb eyes to stare at my nakedness among the beasts still hoping for survival my mother father sisters but already the trains are rolling in the night as I ran beneath the sky a yellow star struck my breast and all the eyes turned away I told him tried to explain how it must have started upstairs they grabbed me and locked me in a box dragged me a hundred times over the earth in metaphorical disgrace while the soldiers chased each other with stones in their hands and burned all the stars in a furnace my survival a mistake he cannot accept forces him to begin conditionally by another form of sequestration pretends to lock himself in a room with the if of my existence the story told in laughter but it resists and recites first the displacement of its displacements leaving me on the threshold staring dumbfounded at the statue of liberty over the girl's shoulder question of selecting the proper beginning he claims then drags me into the tunnel to stare in guilt again between a woman's legs at the triangular cunt of america leads me down the corridor to masturbate his substitution instead of giving me an original experience to deceive the absence of a woman's hand makes believe that I am dead twelve years old when they left me in the primordial closet moment upstairs on the third floor with the old newspapers empty skins seeking unknown pleasure which is only an amorphous substitution thinking that memory is innocent always tells the truth while cheating the original experience the first gesture a hand reaching for the walls to find its proper place since he failed to generate the real story in vain situates me in the wrong abode as I vibrate doubly in his obligation to assign a beginning however sad it may be to my residence here before memory had a source so that it may unfold according to a temporal order a spatial displacement made of words inside his noodling complexities of plagiaristic form I was dead he thinks skips me but I am being given birth into death beyond the open door such is my condition the feet are clear already of the great cunt of existence backward my head will be last to come out on the paper spread your arms voices shout behind the walls I can't but the teller rants my story again and I am alive promising situation I am my beginning in this strange gestation I say I for the first time as he gesticulates in his room surrounded by his madness having once more succeeded in assembling single-handedly the carbon design of my life as I remember the first sound heard in this place when I said I to invent an origin for myself before crumbling into his nonsense on the edge of the precipice leaning against the wind after I placed my filthy package on the roof its warmth still on my hands far away the empty skins already remade into lampshades past moments old dreams I am back in the actuality of my fragile predicament backtracked again into false ambiguities smelling my hands by reflex out of the closet now to affirm the certainty of how it was annul the hypothesis of my excessiveness on which he postulates his babblings his unqualifiable vibration as I register the final absence of my mother crying softly at night my father flushing his blood clots down the sink they threw sand in their eyes struck their back kicked them to exterminate them his calculations yes explanations yes the whole story crossed out my whole family parenthetically xxxx into typographical symbols while I endure my survival from its implausible beginning to its unthinkable end yes false balls all balls ejaculating on his machine reducing my real life to the verbal rehearsals of a little boy half naked trying to extricate himself as he goes on formulating yet another paradox I witness to substitute a guilty gesture for my innocent pleasure call that cleverness oldman to impose on my predicament his false notions of order truth plausibility down the corridor tiptoes now listens to voices murmuring behind the doors refusing that which negates itself as it creates itself both recipient and dispatcher of a story teller told creature on my hands the smell of the package up on the roof to disintegrate in laughter divided I who speaks both the truth and the lie of my condition at the same time from the corner of its mouth to enclose the enunciation and denunciation of what he says in semantic fraudulence because I am untraceable in the dark again as I move now toward my birth out of the closet unable to become the correspondent of his illusions in his room where everything happens by duplication by repetition displacing the objects he wants to apprehend with fake metaphors which bring together on the same level the incongruous the incompatible whereas in my paradox a split exists between the actual me wandering voiceless in temporary landscapes and the virtual being federman pretends to invent in his excremental packages of delusions a survivor who dissolves in verbal articulations unable to do what I had to do admit that his fictions can no longer match the reality of my past me blushing sphinx defecating the riddle of my birth instead he invents me playmates in his chaotic progress for his deficiencies

to tell the truth moinous calls them but let's be honest yes even if
it hurts it is some considerable time now since he last knew what he
is talking about in his flow of wordshit that counterfeits my escape
I dare say as he toys with my fears makes of me a puppet-child whose
strings are entangled rather than letting me be free and spontaneous
to run under the grey canvas sky in search of my present-future then
injects into my eyes a functionless reflexivity but no one is fooled
by his disabused attitude which makes me forget my mother's face her
dark eyes forces me to reshape my father's hopes to convenient usage
for a future life in some far away land subtly hidden into his voice
seeking to vanish again while he thinks words will make me he thinks
his words will eventually stumble on the right aggregate of my being
how clever he would like it to be my fault if his words fail to save
me I resist curious reversal of roles whereby the rustle of his lies
above my head leaves me storyless but through a crack in the wall of
my closet I saw his hand draw a tree and on a branch a bird a scared
mockingbird the shape of a leaf I loved that bird so much that while
my scribbler stared at the sun and was blinded I opened the cage and

hid my heart in a yellow feather to blank his doodling mimicry of my condition which repeats sam's pell mell babel words object without a proper name and inversely named captive of his designs as soon as he stands opposite the space of this flagrant contradiction in the heat of our confrontation but because he failed to substitute himself for the first witness of my beginning he cannot improve his account only reinvents what he thinks really happened on the third floor when the door slammed shut on me summertime escaping into the trees the boots in the courtyard moanings down the staircase my experience retold in false versions inscribed in a fraudulent present-past space that can barely approximate the condition of my voicelessness and so he looks toward the days of my wandering indicating what has been restored by faulty memory how can I progress in deliberate distortions even when the present feeds upon the coming future of this escapee who assumes here his true identity as he decries his own story locked in a space beyond his hands on the periphery of his circular rumbling inside as the selectricstud balls away whirls me in a verbal vacuum pretending to set me free at last in the absence of my own presence no I cannot resign myself to being the inventory of his miscalculations I am not ready for my summation nor do I wish to participate any longer willy nilly in the fiasco of his fabrication failed account of my survival abandoned in the dark with nothing but my own excrement to play with now neatly packaged on the roof to become the symbol of my origin in the wordshit of his fabulation that futile act of creating images of birth into death backward into the cunt of reality regressing toward my expulsion there must be a better way to manifest myself to assert my presence in his exercise-book speak my first words on the margins of verbal authenticity I will step into the light emerge run to some other refuge survive work tell the truth I give you my word resist I will abolish his sustaining paradox expose the implausibility of his fiction with cunning expedients stratagems that will cure him of his madness even if the act of telling my own tale sends him to oblivion his journey to chaos ended his temporary landscapes frozen his visit among the beasts forgotten his real fictitious discourse denounced I will be relentless his exaggerated second-hand tale retold anew with the correct accent all his words obliterated from cambrian brainless algea to his imagination plagiarized head crushed against the wall I will step out of my reversed role speak in my own voice at last even if I must outstretch myself to the unattainable but suppose fatigued and disgusted he abandons me will I be able to emerge alone down the corridor out into the sun will I be able to become the essential and not remain a special event on the edge of the abyss stalled words in regress without destination an historic fiasco within his hysterical screaming obscured by faulty memory yes suppose he gives up dies one morning among millions of unfinished moments in the middle of a word will I remain suspended from his blood lifeless voice within a voice without a story to tell my beginning postponed by federman's absence

now then   I forever been

where to   now   don't even say why   but you

you ask   how   twofold vibration   I

skip   never before spoken   yet what   for me   no

sleep selectricstud hassle stir again in closet upright now unfolded unself movements toward unspeakable future between two refuges alive yet afraid yellow feather boy confined manchild symptom rarely fatal controlled pressure producing typographical hijinx voodoo machines I located in nakedness metaphorically exposed federman out when facing the sun following shadows time again for another book of flights old friend ass in gear detours speak traps crap out symbolic evasions of rebirth this time masturbating no more false closet go run above the stars where tension between peripatetic search for hysterical people makes love unique case unreal america sam no less midwife to unbirth time to admit unredeemed mess accept little boy described fervor not in present retroactive quite never apprehended entirely echoes space of future reinstated in stories only from past images presumed shape reverse of farness stifling faces federman now confront much moinous wordshit start there to provide single voice long dodge closet yet a single word failed logos draws map of journey to chaos evoked a bird here where namredef renders speech burnt out to better question fear realized aspects cancel life digressively movement to touch hands or allow feelings propelling words eventually confront mother now beast father now double sisters too from other side burning stars the felt atrocity in furnace as necessary alchemical fire or both let it burn or neither erased let it go here now again featherless risk of death ultimate helplessness startling puppet fails to fly crafty dodger by props replays old tale artificer of fledging youth in retrospect for remade self caught in unself present as yet unmade unimagined from a soaring echo floating from future to decide discover survival toward shared unwritten life coasting above abyss crossing selectrified eye dissolved issues beyond death duplicating open door tearing the veil of high priestess prepare last scroll played out ready to escape now behind walls sssh necessary energy repulverized pages disaster words threatens unqualifiable babble cheating original experience locked I frantic he cunningly futile primordial elements of flight activities rectifying themselves from different angles useless divergence draws linearity of life undermines word circularity to voices which scream reducible again machine discourse system of recuperation by loss end father now mother seen sisters too measured calculated formulated by typographical symbols within closets correspondence to what again is seen again measured again calculated reformulated xxxx with nearness slight variations to something possible against background of dreams already said already seen foolish pleasures to proliferate in verbal mud to build upon come back retrace already traced lines inscribed a course of action only certitude here in a closet alone outside mystery to be found helplessness of an elsewhere beginning veiled fingers of plagiarism who speaks to whom with neutral voice the questioning lie masks subjects from other stories toward where it dies sometime much wordshit provides single light in closet the threat of becoming just another paradox presence split voice in absentia from failure spoken reconstructs past staging of possible conditionals oldman connects a certitude pretends to offer less said perhaps wanted less trying yet from afar in hollow sound assert itself weakness void rather than an absence force or source previously expected to hear better say admit failure by designating who makes non-existence connivance laughter I unable to invent delegating names anonymous machine in motion scream questions affirmations texture designs negations speculations double or nothing where sun and other stars still burn neither symbols of a beginning nor metaphors microcosm reality gigantic mythocosm edifice of words integrating space figures inside rhetorical perfection name canceled as uttered with balls foutaise again reaches all balls from impossible survival repeat even less than nothing perpetuates itself into future-past region of ruins full circle fingers back into voice prehistoric closet condition doors locked in first refuge plays dead issueless memories erased illusion of existing in excessiveness with cries to infinity in either direction tried to mock silence as rumor hooked to primary self into body splintered fantastically into other versions of real story lingers as alternative traces along diverging tracks of probable digressions onward lessness to endlessness admits reverse of farness equals inverse of nearness in reconciliating four swords piercing armored body by acceptance of youthful defiance with folly sam knows perseverence furthers more shadow box of guilt after newspaper wraps excrement on roof from rolling trains to furnace now remade lampshades runs down staircase to night call of fear smelling hands naked yellow star bird seeks beginning of historic fiasco free at last to journey among the beasts where guts squeaking unfold into laughter from darkness displacement of solitary work recalling front page faces of soldiers staring victorious sphinx defecating his life begins again closet confined as selectricstud resumes movement among empty skins images crumble through distortions spins out lies into a false version leapfrogs infinite stories falling silently into abyss to be replaced by old confusion foretelling subsequent enlightenment by what right a fool echoes from near farness the design of youthful folly for neither darkness fear struggle hopelessness nor resistance makes success symmetry to grasp buried sword reluctant to transgress as he learns to listen be silent accepts bewildered others too exist in closet who seek acceptance not defiance of words naked little boy with hope asks again but to ask again is importunity and here he who importunes receives no answer to importune is folly to strengthen in a fool what is right is holy task as spring wells up at last at foot of mountain face of manchild fosters superior character he knows now by thoroughness in all he does that to go on this way brings madness humiliation childish guilt but good fortune gentleness from devotion to commit transgression for those above negates survival time now to be serious in his closet upstairs no more to speak final solution my truth to say from federman's gelded fingers endlessly here now again

Part II

Discourse and Experiment

8

Toward an Aesthetics of Play and Disruption

*Our poetry now is the realization that we possess nothing. Any-
thing therefore is a delight (since we do not possess it) and thus
need not fear its loss.*
—*John Cage*, A Year from Monday

We possess nothing; rather, we are inhabitants of a world of fictions, a world
constructed by our need for meaning, for stability, for possession. The meanings
we believe grounded in some essential reality are seen to be mere projections of
our desire and hope. Every human act and statement creates a world and estab-
lishes a context of value. But these acts are ultimately meaningless. Their significance lies only in the patterns of desire and belief, or of assertion and doubt, that
they reveal. So that once one is free of the delusions of essential meaning, free
to perceive and self-consciously participate in the free play of the creation and
necessary denial of meaning, one may rejoice, as does Cage, in unrestricted
creativity.

These views, which might be taken for a declaration of postmodernist faith,
are the basis of most recent experimental and avant-garde art. For Cage and the
contemporary writer and artist, art may only claim for itself the goal of self-
reflexive delight in the fragile process of meaning-making; but at the same time,
it must reject any pretension of extrinsic or extensive significance in the meaning
created. It is primarily the process of meaning-making, rather than the ultimate
value of any particular meaning system, that is the subject of contemporary writ-

ing. And appropriately, it is on literature's own being, its creative process and materials, that both the avant-garde and postmodern texts focus.

Ideally, it seems, the contemporary artist's mission is to teach humanity how to play—how to accept and rejoice in the ceaseless game of assertion and deconstruction of aesthetic and social meaning. Displaying itself, the text questions, manipulates, distrusts and distorts itself and its language, yet playfully revels in the dynamics of its creation and transience. Correspondingly, the audience is invited to question, dismantle, and create its own life from the values and patterns of behavior it learns from its culture. This freedom to play—and our art is little if not playful, delightful, and absurd, even in its paranoia—is the *message* of contemporary art, a vague echo of Schiller's dictum: "Man plays only when he is man in the full sense of the word, and *he is totally man only when he plays*."

But if this visionary dimension is implicit in recent art, the playfulness we encounter does seem aggressively elementary. For the writer, the subject and object of play is not man (for "man" is now to be redefined), but language—the words, the grammar, the syntax, the very concept of language. In recent avant-garde writing, as William Burroughs would say, "words float free." They stand out in their self-declared primacy, detached from the things they would refer to, referring instead solely to themselves, or curiously juxtaposed with seemingly inappropriate words or images within puzzling and absurd contexts. Words float free, to be recombined with each other against all rules of logic or syntax, on the one hand suggesting the potential plenitude of meanings arising from a dense overlayering of words and contexts (the legacy of Joyce), or, on the other, intimating the absolute transparency and the artifice of language (the legacy of Stein).

If these words are to float free, however, they must, as Burroughs himself knows only too well, be broken free. For if, indeed, the social languages and values we use are fictions, those fictions are nevertheless formidable. Our culture, our ideology, our collective consciousness and language provide a stability and enclosure that may be illusions, but they are felt by many to be increasingly restrictive, if not repressive. Consequently, the ideal of playfulness in art or social behavior appears to be premature and delusive if it fails to account directly for the *need* for aesthetic and social liberation from the encoded meanings and values of our culture.

For Burroughs and a significant number of avant-garde writers, in fact, such a critique of cultural meaning systems lies at the heart of innovative writing. For them, the writer's apparent freedom is possible only through an aggressive questioning of and assault on society's language. At once humble and presumptuous, the avant-garde writer suggests that literature can only speak for and of itself, yet he declares that the self-consciousness of the creative act is not hermetic but may become a paradigm for all human activity. That is, by illuminating the nature and the limits of aesthetic action, the writer asserts that he or she analogously reveals the workings and tenuousness of all our meaning systems. Rather than culture seen in terms of specific institutions or examples of social behavior, contemporary avant-garde writing describes it as a complex of meaning systems, all of which exhibit the structure and properties of language systems. And once one has recognized the connections among art, language and culture, art can serve as an agent of both liberation and self-creation.

Literature's primary activity, then, is to investigate the nature, limits, and uses of language, and to provide strategies of liberation within them. Self-reflexive art's function, in that language so popular in France and the American academy, is the demystification of language and society's semiotic codes. The writer's disruption of the audience's accustomed reading habits, and the distortion of, or emphasis on, the materiality of language, stimulate if not a practical liberation from the culture's codes of meaning, then at least an individualistic stance within and against those codes, and ultimately an invitation to the audience to assume similar stances.

The innovative writing we encounter today may be both visionary and aggressive. It seeks a self-reflexive, self-sustaining play of consciousness within the medium of language, and at the same time it demands a self-conscious questioning of our inherited patterns of speaking and thinking. To this extent, such an idealistic and antagonistic art affirms the continuity of the avant-garde tradition. Certainly, in this avant-garde the visionary impulse is muted and the aggressive tone barely strident, but it sustains the avant-garde faith that experimentation in the language of art provides new perspectives and knowledge, and that it frees us from established practices of thought and behavior. The linguistic play of the avant-garde today expresses a dual desire: to enable language to say more than it traditionally says, and to make language reveal itself as the medium and shaper of consciousness. The experimentation implies both romantic vision and cultural politics.

9

The Avant-Garde Assault
on Literary Language

While such claims may be made for the contemporary avant-garde, we must return to the fact that the particular focus of avant-garde experimentation severely restricts the art's activist scope and forcefulness. For the avant-garde must face (as must all postmodern artists) the dilemma of the specific limits of an individual's actions within the collective phenomenon of language. As soon as we distort or play with language as a medium, we not only unveil language, but we also threaten to make it incomprehensible or gratuitous, or both. Indeed, surveying the various manifestations of the avant-garde today, we recognize the aptness of Cage's remark: "dealing with language (while waiting for something else than syntax) as though it's a sound-source that can be transformed into gibberish." Certainly, one direction of the avant-garde today involves playing with the phonetic aspects of words, making them possess not meaning, but only sound, even to the point of gibberish. Furthermore, the avant-garde treats language not only as a source of sound, but as a source of visual images. A strong current in the movement, the successor to concrete poetry, treats the word not merely as sign, but as design. Once the word becomes pictorial, or visual, there is little to restrain it from reaching the equivalent of visual gibberish.

Of course, incommunicability has been the danger the avant-garde has encountered for the past hundred years. Each assault on, each freedom taken with language disorients the audience, often to the point of incomprehension. But today, rather than attempting to alter perception and invoke unknown realities, or to use experimental language to describe common if unrecognized phenomena, avant-garde artists play with language in a way that devalues the referential dimension of words. By separating words from what they name in order to stress and manipulate the basic processes of language, writing achieves a degree of abstraction equal to that of the minimal visual artwork (though some of the self-referential linguistic games played, especially in France, suggest that the more appropriate comparison is to conceptual art). In either case, the avant-garde flirts with solipsism, perhaps narcissism, not merely because individual writers establish idiosyncratic styles, but because they demand that the text refer primarily to itself and its self-defining game plan for being. Rather than a recognized reality shared by writers and audience, the audience is offered abstract and often allusive investigations of language.

Individually, then, or within the various broadly defined movements that make up the avant-garde today, the writers presented here explore self-conscious linguistic strategies which critique and play with language primarily by reducing it to its specific elements. This reduction may serve merely to study the essential ambiguity or incompleteness of simple statements (Heissenbüttel); it may accent the sound of phonemes, create words based on dislocated phonemes, or play with words and sounds "hidden" within other words (Jandl, Rühm, Lurie); it may treat the sign as design (Elwert, Helmes); it may locate simple words or concepts within a visual dimension, or make abstract concepts visual (*Poesia Visiva*); it may cause a text to speak about itself or address the audience (Sollers, Roche); or it may play with the malleability and fragility, but also the suggestiveness of language by combining or overlayering several voices and texts at once (Cage/Joyce, Federman).

10
Language as the Subject of Innovative Writing

Once language becomes the explicit subject of experimental literature, the paradoxes inherent in speaking and writing are made manifest. Central to contemporary avant-garde writing, especially in France, are a series of alternating perspectives which the writers insist reveal the inescapable dialectics of discourse: language viewed as the creator of thought, or as the product of thought; language seen as the form, or as the content of thought; as the "spring" or as the "reflection" of the unceasing movement of consciousness; as infinite possibility within finite structure and vocabulary; as definite structure grasped only in an indefinite process. In the most self-reflexive avant-garde texts these abstract processes are given substance through the speaking voice of the text which addresses itself, as subject and form, while addressing its writer and reader.

The resulting abstract texts may reflect the inexact but functional relationship of language (or of the imagination encoded in language) to material reality—language giving voice to a world that it displaces at the same time, reality retreating as it is transformed into discourse, yet haunting and giving unseen foundation to the abstract process. Such a relationship is reflected in the works of Helmut Heissenbüttel, or of Marvin Cohen.

Takahashi Shohachiro's "text for 'to'" and "information sculpture" suggest what might be called an erotics of grammar, a playing against themselves of the various linguistic operations implicit in words, suggesting both the plenitude of language and the arbitrariness of its artifice. In these works he highlights the determination of words' meanings by their linguistic contexts, and the interaction of meanings, contexts, and media.

These writers inquire into the self-sustaining structure of language, questioning what determines it and, conversely, how it determines what is said or thought. For others, these concerns need to be pushed further. Sollers asks, who or what is in control of articulation? Do we speak as the initiators of our language? Or are we spoken *by* language, determined and limited by its structures? Are our thoughts shaped and restricted by the rules and conventions of discourse—a discourse indirectly reflecting the ideology of our culture? Or are we free to fully articulate our desires, our lives? The voice that addresses the reader in his novel *Laws* is language, the language of the text itself. It confronts its listeners as users of language with a claim to de facto priority over them. It is an unsettling, insulting, and subversive claim, an assertion that what we most take for granted determines our conscious thoughts and expression. This immediacy of the apparent non-being of language is the subject of the novel. Here language, the underlying generative force of consciousness, floats free of "reality," addressing itself, manifesting itself, and taking the place of the phenomenal world in the reader's mind. Ironically, this process makes plain the word's fragility and the tenuousness of its power over itself, the world, and its users.

Helmut Heissenbüttel

Mainclausestation

the Something as substratum necessary to thought is the trace of content faded to
an extreme abstraction diminished to the point of a differential otherwise there
could not even be the thought of a Something
Theodor W. Adorno

if you do something with something and even if you're convinced that you can do
something with something something remains something no matter what you do
with something and you get at best something like a paraphrase of something and
then the only advantage would be to realize that even as something like or as
something with which or of which or about which something always remains of
the kind of the category of the index of something and i.e. something remains.

—trans. Rosmarie Waldrop

So Much for Figures

approximately one is not quite two or a bit more than zero approximately two is not exactly two but not three or one either rather something more than one or something less than three or somewhere [infinite possibilities] between one and three etc. of course it gets easier if you go higher [e.g. 50] approximately 50 is perhaps 49 or 51 or 52 or 48 [let's stay away from fractions] well it might even be exactly 50 only I haven't counted or I'm not sure I counted right or I had no time to do it because 50 goes by so fast at any rate it's not likely [this much I can say with certainty] one or infinite

and maybe this is approximately what I can say and by saying I mean that I'm talking about exactly so and so much or about approximately so and so much and i.e. that either I know the figure or I don't but in any case I hold on to the figure as the only true and utterable thing and it's true I can't approximately say what is because if I were to talk approximately I would talk about something which doesn't exist because talking approximately of something exactly so and so much means not only to talk inexactly but you can't even do it because there can be approximately anything which is approximate but my word is my word and my talking is my talking and approximately a word is no word at all but something which dogs do as well or the birds in the sky

approximately one is something more than nothing at all

—trans. Rosmarie Waldrop

Marvin Cohen

What Is the Real, Really? What Does It Mean? Or Do We Only Think It? Is There a Real? But What Is "Is"? And What Does It Mean?

In the early birth of the world, sometime on a former age, there were indeed real things. So many real things existed, reality was formed, on an organized basis. Its proponents worked realistically to this end, and found reward. But when their work was ended, things were no longer real. Only formulations and patterns were, the thoughts and meditations of such. The removal from real things had begun.

Today, meanings are notoriously elastic, and may be stretched to mean anything. Just short of nothing. We debate what is real, and only the debate is real, but not the subjects discussed. And not the things the subjects are about. We have evaded the simple, and built layers of length confounded against absolute elements. Indeed, the real is remote.

How may we re-attain it? Is there magic to enter the real, or merely fundamental simplicity? Of what is a real thing constituted, and by what may we recognize it, as against the sheen of appearance? And when real things are mixed, is it wise to distinguish? Or does wisdom avoid the real?

The real, the real is childish. Is it really so? Yes.

And in the adult world, reality rears its ugly head. Nothing real is left.

Old age, maturity gone to rot, returns to feeble semblances of the real, reverts to foolish sight, a dimming vision of a young and dancing real.

Real, real, come back. "No, I never must." Where will you be, till I find you? "Lost, forever."

The real, the real. If only I had you once more, I would not be writing this. Instead, I would be rejoicing at you. The lovely image of the real. The real itself, mirror-source of the image. The true real, a real devoid of world, empty in the fullness of itself. That real for which we laboriously compensate, piling on. The nature of the real. A real thing, burning in unreality.

The World-Solidifying Imagination

The world does not have enough things in it. This is not a world of everything. To correct that insufficiency, each human inhabitant of what we call the world was provided with the rudiments of imagination. If he's not domesticated, civilized, and cultivated too much in the socialization process, the person's imagination develops beyond its rudiments. When that happens, then, for such an individual, the imagination takes up the slack for the insufficiency of things in the world. His own personal world becomes full. He's art's heir, beauty's heir, everything's heir. History serves him. The human mind becomes a soul. Heaven visits earth, hell visits it too, the myths open up, and yield their joyous secrets.

When that person dies, the world immediately gains more vacuum to replace what that mind had filled it with. A new person gets born of potential. The world greets him with insufficiency. The new person is challenged. Will his mind be equal to all those empty spaces? He fights vacancy, his mind fills. The mind filled, the world is filled—for him. He's the spirit's brother of the one just dead.

Information Sculpture

tezuri 手摺り hand-printed. ～する hand printed. ‖手摺り印刷機 a hand printing press.

tezuri 手釣り hand-line fishing. ‖手釣糸 a hand line.

tezuru 手蔓 ⇨tsute.

ティー 1 [茶] a cup of tea. 2 [ゴルフの] a tee. ‖ティーパーティー a tea party. ティーセット a tea set; tea things. ティーショット a tee shot. ティータイム teatime.

ティーンエージャー a teenager.

ティンパニ a kettledrum; timpani.

to 徒 a party; a company; a gang (悪徒); a set (連中).

to 途 ‖渡欧の途につく leave for Europe. 渡米の途にある be on one's way to America.

to 戸 a door (とびら); a shutter (窓の); a sliding door (引き戸). 戸の取っ手 a door handle (pull). 戸の取っ手振り a doorknob. 戸をあける (締める) open (shut, close) the door. 戸をぱたんと締める bang the door. 戸をたたく knock (rap) at (on) the door; tap (at) the door.

to 都 a metropolis. 東京都 the City of Tokyo. 都の metropolitan. ‖都知事 the Metropolitan Governor; the Governor of Tokyo (Metropolis). 都庁 the Metropolitan Government (Office). 都電(バス) a metropolitan streetcar (bus). 都議会(議員) (a member of) the Metropolitan Assembly. 都民 a citizen of Tokyo. 都民税 the citizenship tax.

-to -と 1 [いっしょに] with. 父と行く with one's father. 2 [および] and. 娘と母 mother and daughter. 3 [ちょうど…のとき] just as; when; the moment…. 家に着くと雨が降りだした It began to rain just as I reached home. It started raining when I got home. 4 [もし] if. 雨が降ると困る If it rains. In case of rain, I keep indoors. 5 […だろうとも] (even) if; even though. 何を言おうと say what you may. 彼が行こうと行くまいと私はかまわない Whether he goes or not, I don't care. 雨が降ろうと風が吹こうと in spite of rain and wind. ⇨-tomo (-とも).

tō 十 ten; half a score. ⇨jū (十).

tō 灯 a light; a lamp.

tō 刀 a sword; a saber; a (surgical) knife (pl. knives) (外科の). 一刀のもとに with one stroke of a sword.

tō 塔 a tower; a steeple (尖塔(せん)). 塔を建てる build (erect) a tower. ‖五重の塔 a five-storied pagoda.

tō 糖 sugar. ⇨tōbun (糖分).

tō 籐 a cane; a rattan. ‖籐椅子 a rattan chair. 籐細工 rattan work.

tō 薹 ‖薹が立つ run (go) to seed; (盛りが過ぎる) be past one's prime; become a has-been (話).

tō 等 1 a grade; a class; a degree. 1(2, 3)等 the first (second, third) class (grade). 1等で行く travel first class. 2 [など] and others; and so on;

---

and so forth; et cetera (etc.). 等々 and so on; and so forth; etc.

tō 当 1 [当を得た] right; just; fair; proper (適当). 当を得た処置 (take) a proper measure. 当を得ている be right (just, fair, reasonable, proper). 2 [この] this; the present (problem); [その] that. 当問題 the matter in question. 当の本人 the person in question. 当の本人は何も知らない He himself knows nothing of it.

tō 党 a party; a clique (閥); a league (同盟); a faction (分派); a coterie (文芸などの). わが党の士 one of our party (set). 党にはいる join a party. 党を組織する form a party (faction). ‖党員 a party member; a member (of the Socialist Party). 党規 party rules. 党三役 the party triumvirate (of the Liberal Democratic Party). 党大会 a party convention. 党役員 a party official. ⇨tosei (党勢), tōseki (党籍).

-tō -頭 ‖牛70頭 seventy head of cattle (head は単複同形).

Tōa 東亜 Eastern Asia; the Far East (極東).

toami 投網(を打つ) (throw) a cast(ing) net.

tōan 答案 [答え] an answer; [用紙] a paper. ～に化学の a paper in chemistry. 白紙のよくできた～ a blank (good) paper. ～を出す hand in one's paper. ～を調べる look over examination papers.

（中略）ある a certain. ～宿にて at an certain inn.

（中略）a shoal; a shoaling. 海が浅くなっている The sea is shallow stance from the shore.

（中略）線 an isobaric line;

tobaku (賭博場).

（中略）gambling; gam（中略）mble away (中略）tur. （中略）で逮捕される red（中略）the act （中略）room, （中略）

tōbaku （中略）ment to overthrow（中略）gawa) shogunate.

tōban （中略）take the plate; take（中略）the mound.

（中略）の者 a person on duty. （中略）か Who is on duty torow? きょうの掃除(そう)は私です It（中略）duty to sweep (the room).

（中略）uri 帳 a drapery; a curtain. （中略）の帳 the veil of night.

（中略）asu 飛ばす 1 [揚げる] fly (a kite); （中略）] fly (a model plane) （中略）blow off. 帽子が～ blow off.

---

horse. 自動車を飛ばして行く hasten (to a place) in a motorcar. 5 [ページなどを] skip (over); jump (a chapter); omit. 次のページを飛ばす We'll skip (over) the next page. ¶デマを～ spread a false rumor. 檄(げき)を～ send out a manifesto.

tobatchiri とばっちり 1 a splash; spray. 着物にかかる get one's clothes splashed with water. 2 [そばづえ] a by-blow. ～を食う get a by-blow; be involved in (a quarrel). 罪のない者に～を受けさせておくわけにはいかない It would not do to have the innocent spattered.

tobatsu 盗伐 secret felling of trees. ―盗伐する fell tress in another's wood lot stealthily.

tōbatsu 討伐 subjugation; suppression. ―討伐する subjugate; suppress; conquer. ‖討伐隊 a punitive force (expedition).

tōbatsu 党閥 a faction; a junto (pl. -s) (政治上の).

tobei 渡米する go (out) to America; visit America. ～の途につく leave (start) for America. ‖渡米視察団 a party (of businessmen) visiting America for inspection.

tōben 答弁 an answer; a reply; an explanation (弁明); (a) defense (被告の). ―答弁する (make) a reply; (give an) answer; explain; [弁護] defend oneself; speak in defense (of). ‖答弁書 a written reply.

tobi 鳶 1 [鳥] a (black-eared) kite. 2 [鳶職] a construction worker. ¶鳶が鷹(たか)を生む 《諺》 "A black hen lays a white egg." 鳶に油揚げをさらわれる have one's share unexpectedly taken by another.

tobi 掉尾の勇をふるう make a final effort or a spurt.

tobiagaru 飛び上がる [空中に] fly (off); soar; [人が] spring (jump) up; jump to one's feet (立つ). いすから～ spring (up) from one's chair. ～ほど痛かった I almost jumped with pain. 飛び上がって喜ぶ leap for joy.

tobiaruku 飛び歩く run about; romp (ふざけて). 金策に～ hustle about to raise money.

tobibako 飛び箱 a vaulting horse.

tobichi 飛び地 [地所] a detached estate.

tobichiru 飛び散る fly about (off) (in different directions); scatter (散乱); splash (水などが).

tobidashinaifu 飛び出しナイフ a switchblade knife.

（中略）1 jump (fly) out. （中略）(rush, burst) out. 檻(おり)か（中略）out of a room. （中略）out of a cage. 庭に（中略）into the garden. 3 [突出] （中略）protrude. ¶田舎(いなか)から～ run away from home (one's country).

Text for "to"

Philippe Sollers

From *Laws*

The entrance teaches us on the spot that it is not nature in itself but the transformations effected by man that are the essential foundations of thought. Within the infinite abbreviation of the particularities of existence I am, if I may say so, the spiral that you reject. The true, we agree, is system, truth is process; but don't expect me to pretend not to be their subject. Divided, fine, that's what I want to be. But also jammed and crammed. The immediacy of my non-being, if I can still express myself in such a way, constitutes my only appearance. My reason that thinks sharpens the differences. What appears to you as the activity of my form is also the very movement of my matter. Does that bother you? Too bad. My dusty necessity does not become freedom because it disappears, but because its identity, still internal, is manifested. Here, among you, in our organic, social nature, together we are witnessing, if you like, the emerging of the concept. Hello there! The syllogism makes me mortal. Only for an instant, obviously. Fundamentally, it is not impossible for me to be the inexhaustible spring of a movement unceasingly being renewed. Spring bothers you, well let's say reflection. The hypothesis is ingenious, not devoid of sadness, however. My negativity that other people find absolute patiently instructs me in dialectic. Whence my indisputable progress in comparison with the babe in arms that I was. In life, my individual subject is separated from the objective. I warn you in advance not to establish my identity as a law, and thus let my contradictory contents fall into the sphere of representation. Kiss me, but quickly. Go where I turn. My greatest extension is also a higher intensity. When I retreat to my simplest depth, how overflowing I am! I blush for it modestly, like a true river. So I proceed towards me by the negativity of the immediate. Briarprongs! Firetongs! Don't envy my fate: it's yours. You are form, and upon that form I shall build my unform. Opposed to the uniform. I am impenetrable, atomic. And you? I am method, I didn't say that I was making a discourse. Still less that I was canvassing for your votes. It's a question of language. Time and space exist outside the moment when I become excessively subjective. I know it, and that's enough help. Take my pulse: tell me if my account is plastic. I could mislead you by insisting on the fact that what begins is already everything by not yet being etc. . . . But in the last analysis. Can matter be absolute form? Is there direct disappearance? What do you think about it? You aren't cold, are you? You want me to cough? My propositions, you've noticed, are animated by a movement by means of which they tend to disappear through themselves. Nevertheless, unity indicates affirmation. Since you have henceforth emerged, I let you add the ineluctable division. Take it and shake it. You can suppress yourself: why should I worry about it? You wouldn't be ashamed to contain my contrary, would you? Everyone appears in the other. So what? This negation rebounds upon us, ricochets off your surfaces. Limit is my quality: wherein I am precision without being obsessed by the substance of our circumcision. My attraction represents the moment of my continuity within my quantity. I'll pattern myself on it. My continuity contains even the discontinuity of my multiplicity, but, so to speak, in a state of complete uninterruption. Some of mine warm me up. Others fill me out. Space is that absolute be(ech) outside of it. Agreed. But let's be cautious. The members of my series, my members in short, should not only be considered as parts of a sum. My movement in relationship to a fraction of space traversed during a certain time presents itself under the different determinations of a movement that is pseudo-uniform, uniformly accelerated, or even, alternatively, uniformly accelerated and uniformly delayed. Don't hope to touch simultaneously my position, my speed. Don't let yourself be entrapped. It's a lovely day. The end, for example, of a fraction of time that represents the duration of the body's fall is itself a fraction of time. My speed exists only in relation to the space traversed in a fraction of time and not to the end of that fraction! A mere nuance!

what am I, who am I, if not certain lines that, in order to form a superficies, should be positioned at the same time as their negation? Lines that are like surfaces, I grant you, but like surfaces that are infinitely thin. The indivisibles in me, notice, are lines when one considers squares, a pyramid, a cone. I restore to them, from time to time, my potential proportion. To the contrary! Suppose that my power, a dubious word, is a plurality of unities, each of which is that very plurality! You see how I maneuver! From that point on, my quantity is, in its truth, my exteriority done to a turn, not indifferent, like having a dish done to a turn, correcting the sauce, increasing the flavor. Imagine a meal without salt, without mustard, without pepper! The fact that I am talking still I excite you more and more. What can I do about it? You try it! This quantity hence is quality itself to the extent that outside this determination quality as such would be nothing. And hop to it! That's right, there's got to be a double passage. A little bit of watering down. Without the second one, quantity would not become the contents of quality, its suppression would be lacking, appreciate the congestion that would flow from it right away. If you're up to the point of conceiving my substantiality in too rigid a fashion, without returning upon itself, you can plan on it that people are going to make fun of you prematurely, too often. My ruse is to attack your existence on the side where its quality does not seem to count! A ruse, all things considered, that is historical. And totally excessive. Date it and transform it. In weight. In volume. My space nonetheless insures the persistence of my dissociated matter. Chemistry could certainly be my language. Music at this point is much closer to me than you perhaps will ever be. Yet your hysteria is understandable. Your deafness too. In compensation my neutrality possesses a combined power of division. Don't invoke the progressiveness of change to explain our appearances, our disappearances. You're being boring, it's a serious matter. Nothing new, thus, nothing unexpected, you're reducing variation, everybody's sick and tired of you. On the other hand my qualitative infinity arises from the flooding of my infinite into my finite, of popular masses into my limited individuality, my overhereness getting out fast, by direct transformation, into my overthereness. And there it is! It's the egg without the dove! Of course, I always manage to fling my unity away from me. Negative, immediate, my tank of essence takes care of the trip. And the ignition. My negation is passage, suppression of passage. The majority, not reaching negation, do not tolerate, it's normal, the negation of negation. That is, they hesitate in affirmation. Which is my friction. What rhythm! Harmony! No one knows if I'm coming back, if I'm leaving. Source of supplementary pleasure. And of frantic denials. The best of them reinforce me. They

118

kill me, it's true, but better and better. And thus my proverbial immediacy presents itself under the form of return, constitutes again the negative that is the appearance of beginning whose return itself constitutes negation. That's my vice! This return into oneself is of course simultaneously suppression of self, your favorite hide-and-seek in short, and as your reflection is pushed away, your repulsion, for its part, comes to be equivalent to your return. The same thing is true of your pluming and its pulsing in your crooning, since there aren't any foxes or woods anymore. Having said that, you are free to consider yourself as the bearer of quality, which is the unequal of negation. The form of this proposition can be considered as the hidden necessity consisting in adding still more movement to this abstract identity. It is my right, once again. The whole difference is there: nothingness expressed in language. You can add: the equal and the unequal are their own unequal. I'm equally indifferent. I am also the contrary existing by itself. In position! Very much in position! I am what the positive should be. Like light! No less, no more. Here. Not-here. Basicsubstanceitself. Recoil! Inothingness. When I emerge, plop! The reflection blasts apart. I depart in the blasts. It is very simple: inasmuch as I am a base, I am distinguished from form, while being at the same time substance and one moment of form. I have reflected on it a lot! It's true, without folderol. Perhaps my behavior in spite of everything is too negative in respect to myself. Truly? I can do nothing about it: my matter is form in itself. It's stronger than I am. There's nothing formal about all this. Even less, anything formalist. It's an instantaneous association. If you liberate it, you understand it. If not, not. The thing conditions itself and brings itself to its conditions. Abyss! Crew and cargo sunk! This. These. Those. That-that. I confess: I have as a base only my own nullity. My porosity penetrates me. The existing world rises up tranquilly within me to become a tempestuous reign of laws! At both poles! Conversation with causation! In practice! And in theory! Happy to have you aboard, reader, but remember there aren't thirty-six conductors in the subway. Don't stick your cock out of the window, don't make any obscene signs with your hemorrhoids, let's flow into the lubricated, and if a sector gets too physical, you can stick your foot up his ordinator.

—trans. William H. Matheson and Emma Kafalenos

119

11

Literary Disruption as the Basis of Creation

The avant-garde seeks not merely to make language the subject of literature, but to distort that language in order both to prohibit the customary use of words and to create new patterns of linguistic interaction. Traditionally, the processes of criticism and disruption have played major roles in avant-garde works, as countless avant-garde writers and artists have declared the act of aesthetic negation the necessary prelude to creation. In the contemporary avant-garde, the act of potential transformation—both destructive and creative—becomes the explicit focus of the text. The writer attempts to disconnect, erase, or cut up the normal flow of words, accentuating particular syllables, words, meanings, or linguistic rules while at the same time obscuring others. Language, syntax, even the graphics of word and text are fair game, to be disrupted and reorganized into visual and linguistic patterns whose new meanings can only be suggested.

For example, Takahashi Shohachiro, who points to the play of an individual word and its contexts on the one hand, rips words free from their contexts on the other, in order to suggest new frameworks. (Or perhaps, in the pieces that follow, words only intimate playfully another view of their original context.)

Scott Helmes takes the disruption of language to an extreme, erasing and blurring words and letters, in some pieces leaving only graphic representations of the process of negation-creation, in others making artful designs that tease the reader into seeking possible lingering messages.

John Cage breaks down an existing literary structure, to create in these mesostics the literary equivalent of his randomly structured sound performances. Entering that already polysemous and confusing work, *Finnegans Wake*, he finds the first words on each page that present him with the letters to spell out Joyce's name, thus creating a new text which disrupts the profuse meanings of the novel but which has no meaning other than that of homage to Joyce and a celebration of art and language.

Takahashi Shohachiro

Poems Fall (Three Versions)

がふってくる

Scott Helmes

Six Untitled Works

128

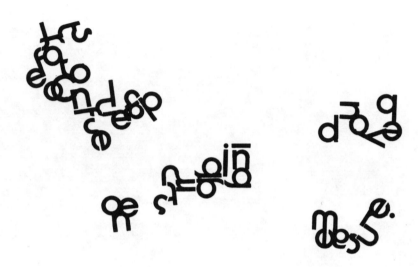

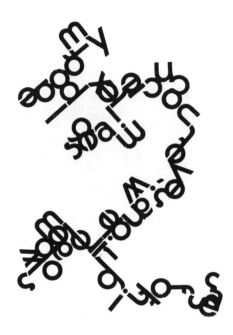

130

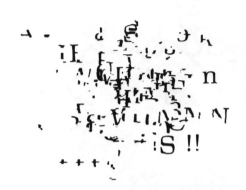

John Cage

Writing for the Third Time Through Finnegans Wake

I

131

wroth with twone nathandJoe   3

A

Malt

jhEm

Shen

pftJschute

Of finnegan

that the humptYhillhead of humself

is at the knoCk out

in thE park

Jiccup   4

the fAther

My shining

thE

Soft

                    Judges
               Or helviticus
          sternelY
          watsCh
          thE

                    Jebel   5
               And
          it May half
          havE
          hiS

          derryJellybies   6
               arOund
     and thurum in fancYmud
          ereCtion dimb
          hE

               fJord
          his bAywinds'
               hiM
          thE livvylong   7
          innS

                    Jamey
               Our   8
          paddY
          is a ffrinCh
          thE

in Jun
is the crimeAline of
the three lipoleuMs this is
thE
book of Stralegy

the Jinnies is
willingdOne
sneaking his phillippY
dispatCh
to irrigatE

Jinnies
to fontAnnoy
the lipoleuMs
thE
iS gonn

cherry Jinnies
figtreeyOu
damn fairY ann
tiC for
mE

Jinnies
A sip
lipoleuMs
thE
thiS

9

Jinnies cry
gOat
rinning awaY to
belChum's
platE for citchin

Jinnies
brAnlish
lipoleuMs
spy on thE
from hiS

waxing ranJymad
fOr
hneY
and pumpim Cry
thE

Jig-
A-
Month
and onE
Such

Jist
dOes
till bYes will be
fliCk
flEckflinging

10

11

                    Job   12
                  bAndy
                   May
                  takE
           two moundS

                  muJical   13
                   bOx
                  mirY
              of the inCabus
                  usEd   *135*

        mammon luJius
          in his grAnd
          historioruM
              wrotE
            annalS f.

        thrown up Jerrybuilding   15
                  tO
             the citY
       thangas vain have been Confusium
            hold thEm

                  kopJe in pelted thongs
                   A
                  pigMaid
              hoagshEad
                  Shroonk

it Junipery
Or
febrewerY
marraCks
or alEbrill or

Jute
let us swop hAts
Mutt
jutE
whoat iS the mutter with you mutt

Jute
tO be
You
hasatenCy urp
i trumplE from

Jute
one eyegonblAck
Mutt
how woodEn i not
old grilSy

Jute
Our
bY
bull on a Compturf
rEx

Jute
boildoyle And
weird froM sturk to finnic
onhEard of
and umScene gut aftermeal

Jute
babylOne the
seemeterY
whiCh iz
jutE   18   *137*

Jute
the gyAnt forficules with
Mutt
jutE hwaad
you aStoneaged

Jute
yOu
You
this Claybook
this allaphbEd

of obJects   19
dollies Alfrids
corMacks and
arE
See the

ivargraine Jadesses with a message
in their mOuths and
saY too us to be
niCk
sons of thE sod sons

Jined   20
mAy his
Mud
sundEr
it cloSeth

and Jarl van   21
up in his lamphOuse
laYing
Cold hands
on himsElf and his

Jiminies
And
be derMot
thE
of hiS inn only the

Jiminy
tristOpher and
the shandY westerness
baCk
to my Earin stop   but

Jiminy
soAp
hiM
and shE
So

again at Jarl
Of samers
and the jiminY with her
in their first infanCy
bElow

Jiminy
And
jiMiny and
thE
lilipath wayS to

rain and Jarl
vOn
mY
laurenCy night of
Erio and

Jiminy
And
Monitrix to touch
shE
allSecure and he became a

Jarl
vOn
larrYhill
for the third Charm
and jarl von hoothEr

Jiminy toughertrees
And
trihuMp asking
thE
triS why do i am alook alike

acoming with a fork lance of lightning Jarl
vOn
arkwaY of his
Chollar and his allabuff
and his bullbraggin soxanglovEs and his

Jimminies   23
wAs
nickylow Malo
bE
Silex

Jerusalemfaring   26
in arssia manOr
You had
worms and sCalding
vEstray

Just
A
postMan's knock
round thE
diggingS and

a Jerry
sOmetimes
hettY
a Child of mary

shE'll

do no Jugglywuggly
with her wAr souvenir
Murial
assurE
a Sure there

12

Play and Performance in the Avant-Garde Text

What has been separated, randomly pulled apart, or partially erased can be re-assembled in meaningful, gratuitous, or even purposively nonsensical patterns. The result may be carefully contrived artifices of beauty, or verbal and visual gibberish. The mode of such creation is that of play—of (re)creation. The written text becomes a performance in which the process of creation is often more significant than the resulting artwork. As in contemporary music and dance, chance structures and non-essential elements may achieve primary status. Disparate linguistic elements, freed from their referential contexts and syntax, become the total content of the work.

In such configurations, in sound or visual performances, what meaning exists? We can speak of the meaning of the process of creation, but can we determine the "meaning" of any individual text? Often the works seem absolutely hermetic, self-contained artifices in which meaning arises solely out of the fragments of linguistic elements and the arbitrary visual organization established by the writer, or between the semantic and aural interplay of the syllables and words. In all of the works that follow, as in so many avant-garde texts today, the strangeness of the text points to its arbitrary origin. It asserts the writer's freedom to seek new modes of signification by ripping apart the basic elements of language in order to rearrange them in apparently incomplete and discordant patterns out of which unexpected meaning might emerge.

Ernst Jandl and Gerhard Rühm make games out of spelling and printing, juxtaposing words within words or (in Rühm's case) shifting the visual focus from one way of reading a word to another—in effect, creating a literary equivalent of op-art.

Or the visual emphasis may shift to the aural, and the play with words may become a game of phonemes that suggests the performance aspects of the verbal text—especially in some of Jandl's and Lurie's works.

Ori and Elwert, on the other hand, use the idea of performance to create visual structures of letters, words, and images.

Ernst Jandl

third try successful

he tries to put a bulthroughlet his brain
he tries to put a bthurloulghet his brain

he puts $\left\{ \begin{array}{c} \text{a} \\ \text{through his} \end{array} \right\}$ bburlalient

gestures: a game

weather ye poses

1

145

```
crawl
c raw l
c  raw  l
c   raw   l
c    raw    l

champ
c ham p
c  ham  p
c   ham   p
c    ham    p
```

2

```
anglican
```

for a piss-hop

```
bluesy
b lues y
b  lues  y
b   lues   y
b    lues    y
```

3

```
      truth
   t  rut h
   t  rut  h
   t  rut    h
   t   rut     h
```

4

```
      heart
   h  ear t
   h  ear  t
   h  ear   t
   h   ear    t
```

146

```
      mouth
   m  out h
   m  out  h
   m   out   h
   m    out     h
```

5

for mack the naif

```
      chimp
   c  him p
   c  him  p
   c   him   p
   c    him     p
```

```
      muse
   m  us e
   m  us  e
   m   us   e
   m    us     e
```

Gerhard Rühm

leafleafleafleafleafleafleafleafleaflea

/

Ernst Jandl

schtzngrmm

```
schtzngrmm
schtzngrmm
t—t—t—t
t—t—t—t
grrrmmmmm
t—t—t—t
s————c————h
tzngrmm
tzngrmm
tzngrmm
grrrmmmmm
schtzn
schtzn
t—t—t—t
t—t—t—t
schtzngrmm
schtzngrmm
tsssssssssssssssssss
grrt
grrrrrt
grrrrrrrrrt
scht
scht
t—t—t—t—t—t—t—t—t—t
scht
```

tzngrmm

tzngrmm

t–t–t–t–t–t–t–t–t–t

scht

scht

scht

scht

scht

grrrrrrrrrrrrrrrrrrrrrrrrrrrrrrrrr

t–tt

chanson

l'amour
die tür
the chair
der bauch

the chair
die tür
l'amour
der bauch

der bauch
die tür
the chair
l'amour

l'amour
die tür
the chair

le tür
d'amour
der chair
the bauch

le chair
der tür
die bauch
th'amour

le bauch
th'amour
die chair
der tür

l'amour
die tür
the chair

am'lour
tie dür
che thair
ber dauch

tie dair
che lauch
am thür
ber'dour

che dauch
am'thour
ber dür
tie lair

l'amour
die tür
the chair

calypso

ich was not yet
in brasilien
nach brasilien
wulld ich laik du go

wer de wimen
arr so ander
so quait ander
denn anderwo

ich was not yet
in brasilien
nach brasilien
wulld ich laik du go

als ich anderschdehn
mange lanquidsch
will ich anderschdehn
auch lanquidsch in rioo

ich was not yet
in brasilien
nach brasilien
wulld ich laik du go

wenn de senden
mi across de meer
wai mi not senden wer
ich wulld laik du go

yes yes de senden
mi across de meer
wer ich was not yet
ich laik du go sehr

ich was not yet
in brasilien
yes nach brasilien
wulld ich laik du go

Toby Lurie

Color Improvisation
for three voices

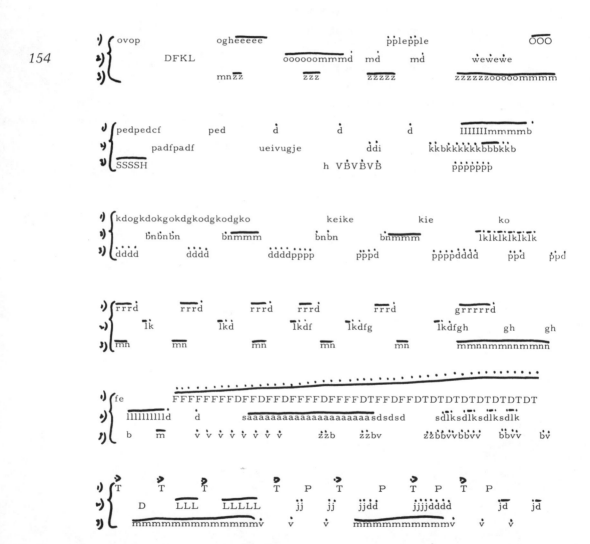

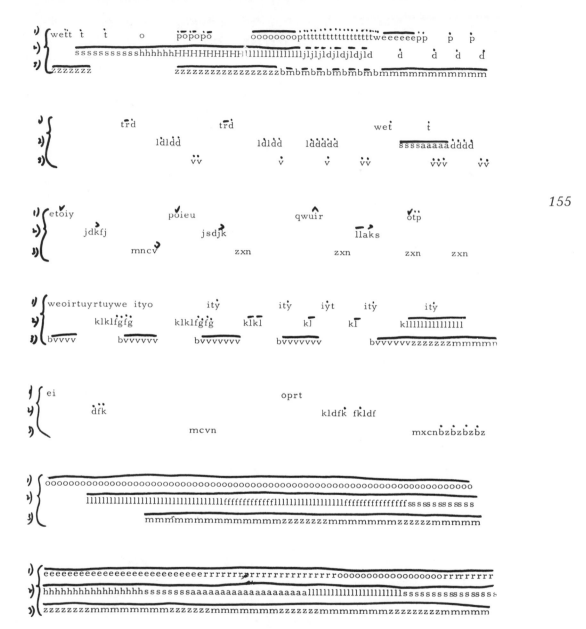

155

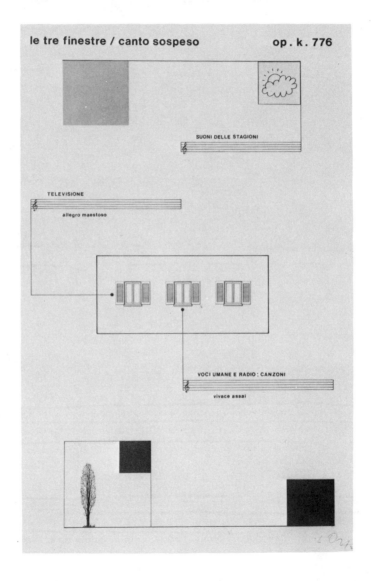

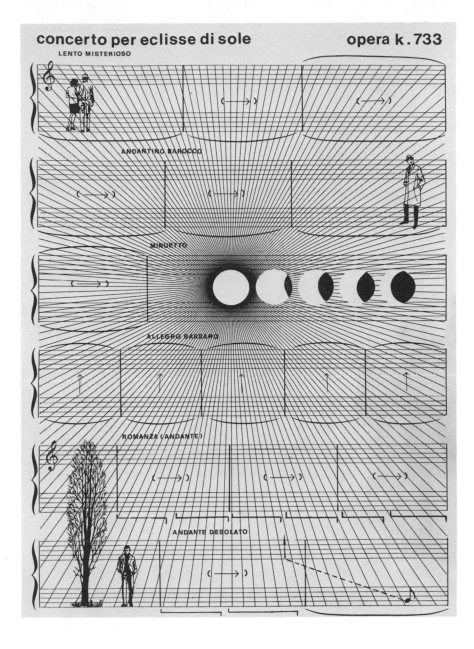

158

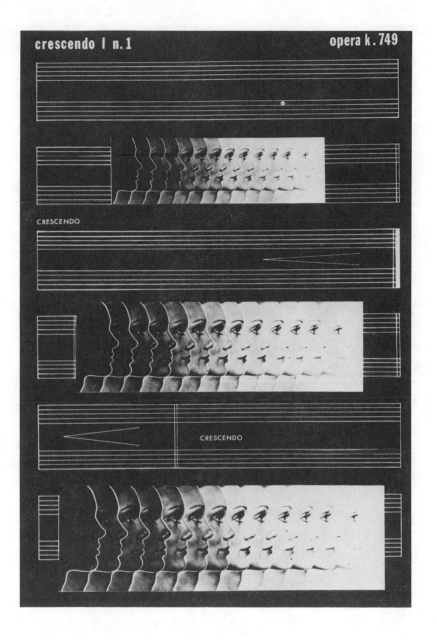

159

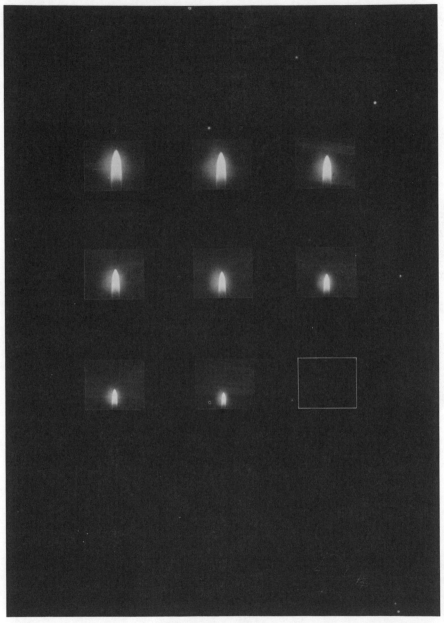

Narrazione Aperta

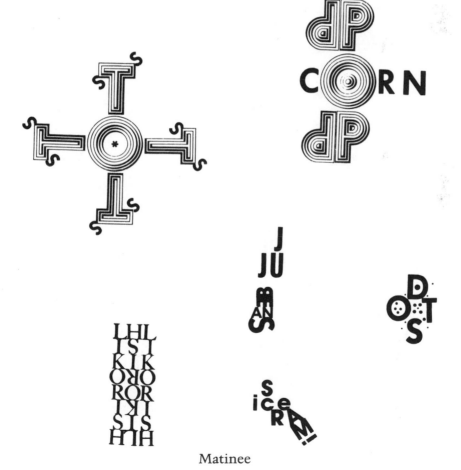

Matinee

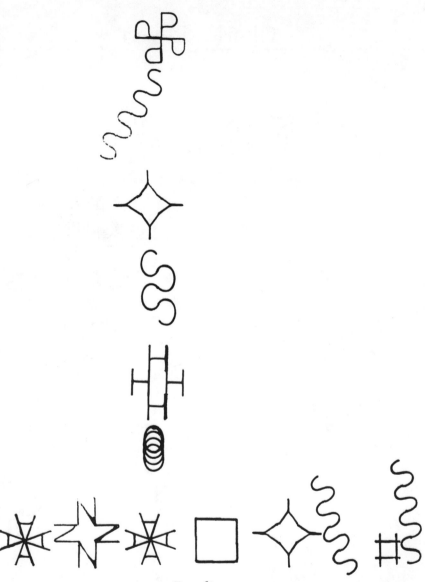

Freudian

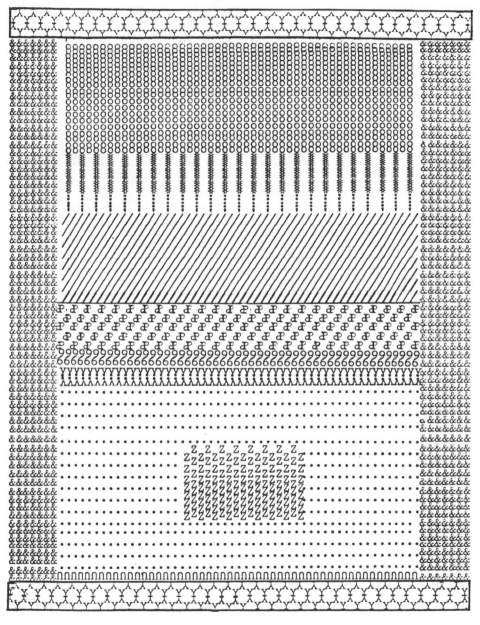

Roman Atomizer

13
Visual Poetry

Words float free. Having become new words, new texts, new performance, they float free to join new contexts—visual images. Words combine with images; are they searching for new referents? If so, the connections never seem securely achieved, for Poesia Visiva—visual poetry—creates an inter*play* of text and image independent of both literature and the visual arts. Neither art form assumes a privileged status, but each contributes to what may be a new form of metaphor, based on disjunctive but complementary images from two different modes of perception.

Poesia Visiva is an international movement, though centered in Europe, Japan, and the United States. Already represented in this collection by Arias-Misson, Takahashi, and Ori, the movement embraces writers whose specific thematic concerns may vary—some will be discussed in the next section on politics—but who share with Valoch and Miccini (perhaps the most traditionally aestheticist poets) a concern for the semantic possibilities of the visible, and the visual dimension of the concept.

In these works, language is treated both as abstraction and as pure sign. The "immediacy of its non-being" and the dominion of language over phenomena are both alleged and undermined by the insistence of the visual subject. Together, the word and the image provide the basis for a new series of performances, meditation, and play.

Jiri Valoch

Building Piece

Forest Poem

About Memory

168

Esse

Rosa Rossa

Poesia

τέσσαρα γὰρ πάντων ῥιζώματα πρῶτον· Ζεὺς ἀργὴς...

Fuoco
"For there are four roots of all things: Zeus the bright"

Part III

The Social Text

14

The Social Extension
of Literary Discourse

Since language, the basis of literature and society, is the subject and object of recent avant-garde experimentation, the patterns of play and disruption that characterize contemporary writing can suggest both a radical aesthetic vision and a political dimension. The specific foci of avant-garde innovation—the materiality of words, the grammar and syntax of language, the shaping of personal voice, and the determinants of collective discourse—all indicate an intention to alter the fundamental relationships between the writer and the audience and between the individual and society. What is ultimately at stake here is a reorientation of the manner in which individuals understand their connection to society—how established linguistic and conceptual patterns determine individual and social behavior, and how individual action may alter those patterns.

Certainly, it is evident from many of the works in the preceding sections that much of the recent avant-garde manipulation and distortion of language expresses no explicitly formulated political consciousness. It is significant, however, that these disruptive experiments are not the actions of an isolated group of writers; nor do they define a single literary methodology or focus. Rather, as the representative texts of this collection reveal, the avant-garde's self-reflexive linguistic disruption and innovation is a worldwide and extremely varied phenomenon. That phenomenon should be placed in two larger contexts, that of postmodernism's exploration of the nature and workings of literary and social sign systems, and that of structuralist and post-structuralist criticism's radical semiological analyses of our society's discourse and ideology. When considered in such contexts, these works testify to a widespread unsettled state of literary and social consciousness.

But these contexts and literary activities have developed only recently and are still in the process of defining themselves. They provide the stimulus for continued disruptive probing of literary practice, but do not as yet offer a clear direction for literary development. Furthermore, in the absence of a well-defined and vital movement of political radicalism today, the individual avant-garde work tends to fall back upon itself. It locates, in the process of creation, an expression of the complex interaction of the writer's use of language and society's codes of meaning and value; in addition, it discovers in that creative process an aesthetic and essentially private resolution of the sense of conflict between individual desire or action and social reality.

If a political stance is implied here, it is that of anarchism, itself a long-standing tradition of individualistic rebellion and idealism that the literary bohemians and intelligentsia have exhibited for the past century and a half. The anarchist spirit of recent avant-garde writing asserts that the writer's freedom must be created in the present moment by the innovative work—a work which disrupts the authority of convention and makes the improvisational process of self-conscious creation its primary value. The message of utopian anarchists like John Cage is that writers and individuals must act as if, by the very force of personal desire, they were already free, for in the creative process they will discover their only freedom, the freedom of playful self-creation with blatant disregard for the given conventions of artistic and social behavior. Such an ideal of self-creation, based as it is on disruption, improvisation, and self-reflexive analysis, signals a social antagonism. But rather than implying a confrontational political stance, it suggests a more problematic model for rewriting the rules of literature and society by its willingness to limit itself to apparently gratuitous creative play without concern for traditional political theory, and by its efforts to turn the "felt ultimacies" of experience—personal fragmentation, repression, and vulnerability—into the basis of new forms of personal and collective anarchic behavior.

Most avant-garde works, then, express a double vision—one turned outward toward the social context that defines the terrain of individual action; the other turned back upon itself, seeking the power of personal freedom and desire. Each insists on the primacy of the personal moment, but beyond this moment, many contemporary avant-garde texts attempt to address directly the ideological extensions of their personal actions in language and society. Generally, two tendencies are evident among those writers who insist on the political significance of formal innovation. One presents traditional political images or themes within a new aesthetic style. The writers explore the possibilities of the new technique, but remain committed to a direct message inherited from political theory or social experience. The visual poet Paul de Vree, for example, combines verbal and visual images to highlight a social critique of all-too-familiar exploitation and oppression. Amiri Baraka, schooled in the modernist tradition of poetics, now criticizes the elitist presumptions of most formal experimentation. He continues to accept the concept of the avant-garde, but insists that innovations in poetic language be directed toward the working and exploited populace, and that they communicate in accessible language complex ideas based on Marxist-Leninist thought.

The second tendency engages in formal experimentation in order to explore the ideological significance of the relationship between personal language and social codes of meaning. Writers such as Sarduy, Roche, and Sollers assert that the self-reflexive text need not restrict itself to its linguistic or literary framework; such a text may also illuminate and call into question the operation of the larger semiotic codes of this culture, codes of which literature is only one form. But by extending the fragmenting vision and improvisational playfulness of aesthetic creation to the political domain, these texts do not repress the essentially anarchic, self-centered spirit of avant-garde activism. Rather, they demand that the political sensibility be "rewritten"—that our means of perceiving and responding to cultural limitations be revised along the lines of the writer's dynamic relationship to the text, literary discourse, and his or her self-expression. The avant-garde text thus strives self-consciously to position itself and its audience within the superstructure of society, which it calls the "social text." In so doing, it seeks an as yet unformulated freedom of self-reflexive creation and action, even as every self-conscious action reveals the limits of personal power, knowledge, and vision within the oppressive framework of that social text.

15
The Social Text

The social text is a web of meaning systems that manifest themselves in patterns of personal and collective behavior, values, desires, fears, perception, and expression. The ideological structures which surround us seem to be vast, powerful, but often obscure texts which (if we could interpret them) would prove to be the origin of much of the aggression and paranoia, the individual fragmentation and ambiguity, and finally the sense of irrelevant freedom that characterize the personal context.

The writer may merely point to the disturbing collage of words, images, texts, and contexts, as does Shimizu Toshihiko. He may find himself walking through and being enveloped by a text and a political context, as does Alain Arias-Misson. The individual may thus find himself demeaned by and irrelevant to the conflicts of languages of power—but he might also discover the opportunity to play with those languages and to demystify them at the same time.

Lucia Marcucci juxtaposes personal, corporal images against images of established power systems—governmental, financial, artistic, sexual—and creates a tension in which the feminine is subjected to the domination of cultural ideologies, even as it undermines their presumed authority.

And Toby Lurie's chant of letters sings of the none too benign embrace of "CIA" and "I."

Shimizu Toshihiko

Creep

Popcrete Poem

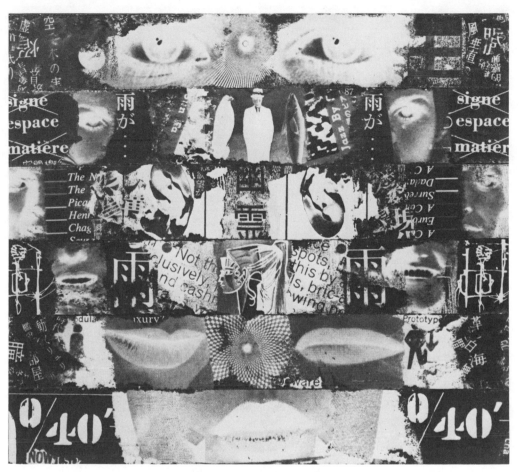

Counter-World

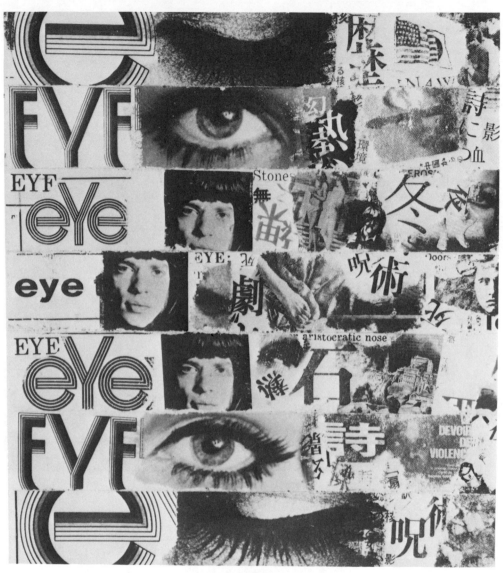

Eye Poem

Alain Arias-Misson

Narrative Series on a News Item on the Arab-Israeli Conflict

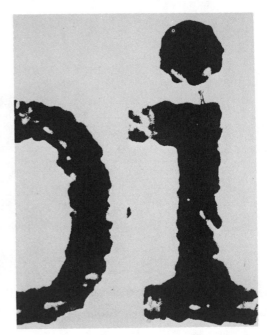

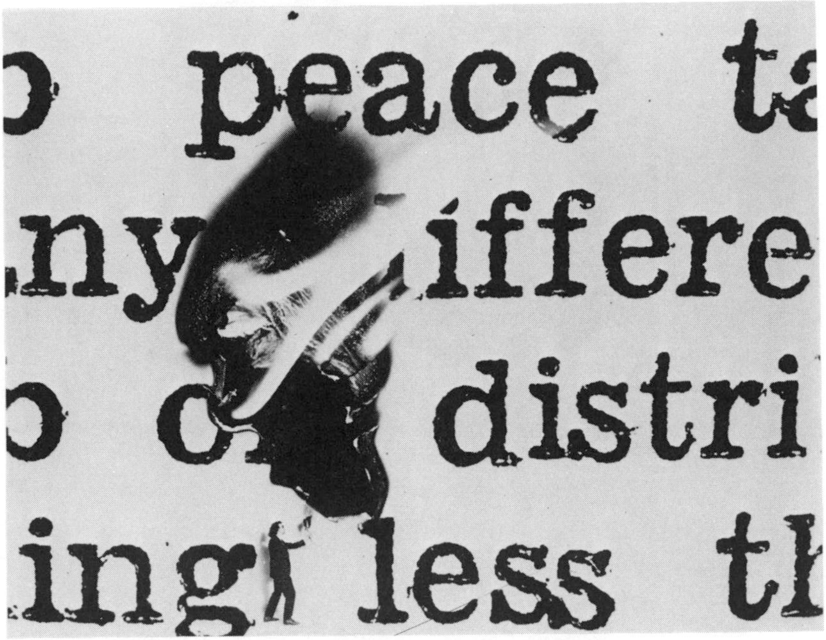
peace
less

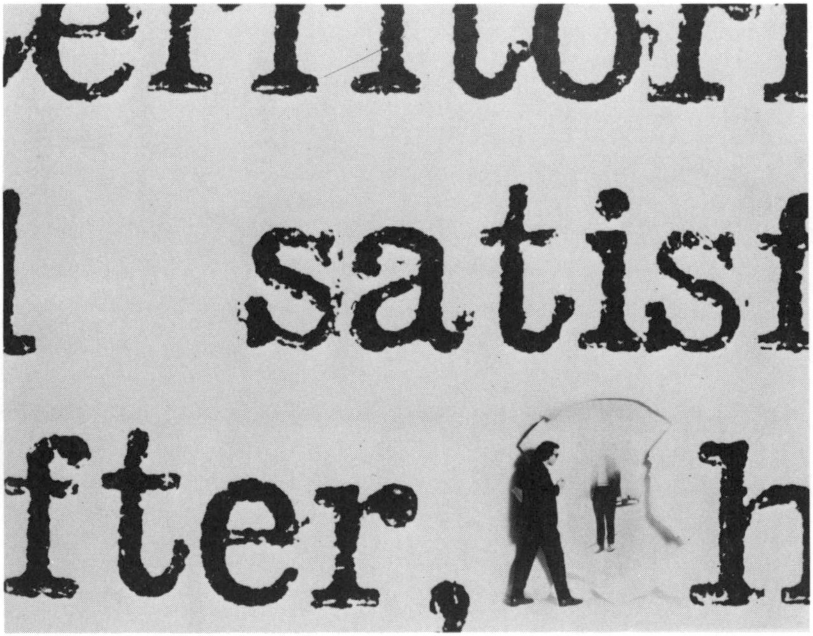
erritor
l satisf
fter, h

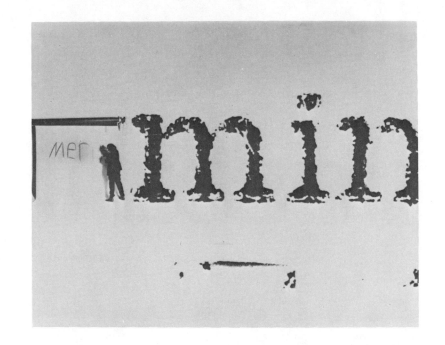

ritories.

But he warned that
coming Israeli-Arab pe
would not make any
to the present Arab oil
tion policies. Nothing
the complete evacuatio
Palestinian territories
Israelis would satisfy
said. Thereafter, he
permanent peace treaty
the Arabs and Israel
sible.

Lucia Marcucci

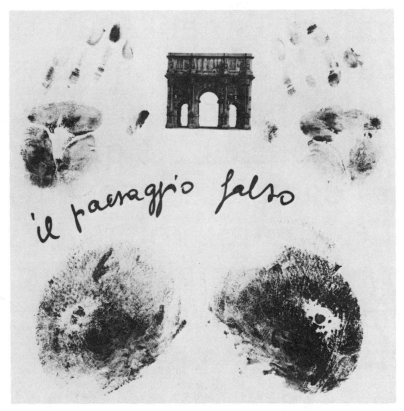

Il Paesaggio falso

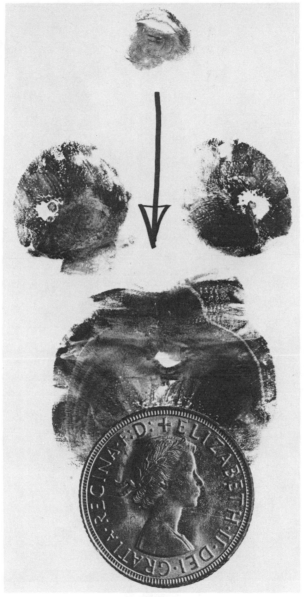

Dei Gratia

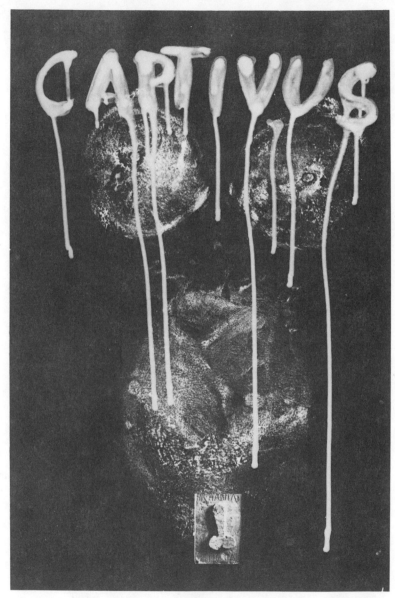

Captivus

Culturae

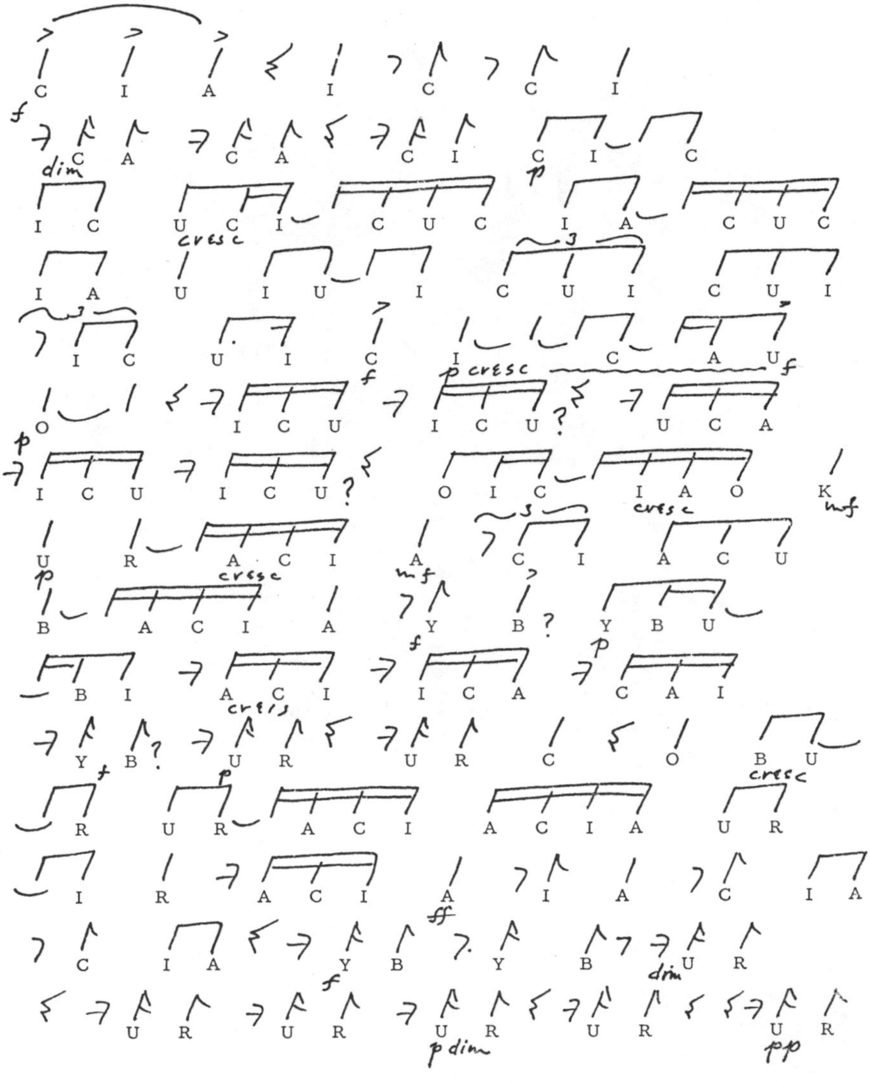
C I A I C C I
C A C A C I C I C
I C U C I C U C I A C U C
I A U I U I C U I C U I
I C U I C I C A U
O I C U I C U ? U C A
I C U I C U ? O I C I A O K
U R A C I A C I A C U
B A C I A Y B ? Y B U
B I A C I I C A C A I
Y B ? U R U R C O B U
R U R A C I A C I A U R
I R A C I A I A C I A
C I A Y B Y B U R
U R U R U R U R U R

16

The Writer in Language and Ideology

Self-consciously situated within language, as well as within society and its semiotic codes, the avant-garde writer confronts the limits of individual innovation imposed by literary practice. What we can say is determined by the shared conventions of language. Even though several writers in this anthology willfully push their works beyond comprehensibility, most operate within or at the boundaries of accepted literary conventions, even as they struggle to change those conventions.

Each avant-garde innovation thus represents, to some extent, a battle in language, literature, and society between the already spoken and the as yet unspoken. The contemporary writer recognizes, however, that even what has not been said is a latent element of the given system of discourse, and is consequently limited in its potentially disruptive power. Furthermore, the individual writer is not the sole origin of the new; he only serves to set in motion the dynamics of change already prefigured within the linguistic—or political—system. The writer is already shaped by the language he or she uses, since self-expression and creation depend on established discourse. Consequently, every effort to subvert literary practice threatens to further undermine an already vulnerable sense of self-possession. The avant-garde writer still seeks to make explicit and to aggravate the inherent tendencies of linguistic dynamism, change, and semantic profusion within literary language, to provide a model for disruptive and creative action within any given semiotic system, whether literary or social.

In contemporary writing, the most common practice is to use distortion, fragmentation, parody, and exaggeration in order to accent the weaknesses of particular meaning systems and to make a given literary or political context work against itself. The languages around us are never totally established, never fully in command of themselves or of us, the avant-garde declares. Like all discourse, languages of power strive for completion and authority, but they remain unstable, ambiguous, and vulnerable. Consequently, to disrupt or make evident the complexity and radical arbitrariness of language is said to be the individual's most effective means of achieving personal (and perhaps collective) freedom and articulation.

Undermining language, but also being undermined by his or her own actions, the avant-garde writer cannot offer alternative systems of belief or meaning. Such systems would only threaten to become different versions of ideology, both betraying their radical origins and being vulnerable to further disruptive literary action. The avant-garde text thus challenges the meaning systems that surround it and that give it contextual meaning. In the resulting disruption of definite meaning, it hopes to discover its own reward of anarchic, if problematic self-creation.

In the following sections from the novel *Laws*, Philippe Sollers's satiric presentation of a chain of opposing ideologies—religious, Soviet, capitalist—and his rather didactic portrayal of an aesthetic-revolutionary position presume to be revolutionary in two ways: first, by satirizing the authoritarian and sexual fixations of the conservative ideologues; second, by Sollers's own play with language, which suggests the (Joycean) malleability and plenitude of words. Strangely, in this section, the revolutionaries speak in the most direct language. Sollers believes himself to be offering examples of a critical and productive language; that is, for him, as for other avant-garde writers, self-reflexive language announces itself as a form of direct political activism. Language, he declares, can never be taken for granted merely as a convenient tool to articulate a "revolutionary" message. Rather, it must be seen as a process which acts in society and which has its own record of historical change, the result of continuous personal and collective action within discourse. Language at any given moment embodies its culture's ideology. For that ideology to be changed, language itself must be altered.

Sollers believes that some positive alternative to existing ideologies can be created through revolutionary aesthetics and social action. That belief clearly is not shared by other avant-garde writers, who are content to satirize the absurdities of those ideologies and of avant-garde utopianism. Helmut Heissenbüttel, for example, offers stringent portraits of the antagonism at the heart of political behavior, but he does not privilege any particular position. Instead, he leaves us with an ironic evocation of utopia, here in the universal acclamation of a communist future. Gerhard Rühm, in a simple design, similarly suggests the cramping, destructive results of political banding. Lucia Marcucci offers another ambivalent vision of poetry's romantic theme—revolution—which both validates and satirizes the political aspirations of the avant-garde.

Philippe Sollers

From *Laws*

what's important in all that if you ask where are we what's happening what's the question is the pages' overflowing with your concrete life made half-concrete before behind you and on the sides sensation of sailing out of the margin mild vertigo not real scalding your ankles great historic murmur nature's yours globule kite subject that's tragic irreversible etc. . . . but sharp laughter that leaves you amelt. And makes you amused. Asked the correspondence in homo of ludic behavior in the animal dog in the field chasing its tail or its shadow answer: homo slavers whiter in the weather. Not to mention the commitment. Against reoccurring obstructions jugjug housepainters breeders of stoolpigeons bloodthirsty colonels farting. Against starspangled police on every shore. Clearly nothing to understand unless you dear navel consider that the people alone and their languages are and constitute the author who gets out of it himself only by reflecting that aspiration movement. His voice returns to froth that cries. Where hearing lies. Sound the trumpet. Saaound. Till araound. Ah, egopolise! Attention, police! Politics concentrated expression of the economy. For murmuring into music, mimi. And from monkey to the old man inspecting the sheath defending unguilty somberobed mama for cock-sacking. (H)elmet! Below his undernose bringing back his ball shafted vibrated and drizzling again. Oh frenum of the tongue! Millions of leaves pouring it out series holding his mother who's slowing up. Every sign in frieze-repetition. Eyes cones rods upon the blue housings its retina in position. And hemophilia. Names that finally get to hands all wet, grains in gobs in put-up jobs. Gray matter drunk as a hatter. Flabby lobes. Ganglions lesions in the holes. I've a good brain in my anthro crane. The problem is those fashits easily stick electrodes in you playing psychiatry schlack social fascists likewise. Imagining themselves mystified by the machine. Butchers to make you talk sex auricle. I see you haven't completely measured the gravity of the times hospital prison compulsory syntax wasn't antonin electrocuted in seclusion? Cousin, that calls for recusion? And he's stuck again in a nanosecond. His sounding. The tale in the hall of a sanguinary soul buried alive in a wall. The pouched pocket cavern animosipainandhurt in his huntforever'n pack me more pain. Round and round it goes, and where it stabs nobody knows. The word's way is in the mattair and if he says those two haven't ever been bored he's famous for his farce for the multifarious. The sole real system is sudden. Dispensed with derm. Exempted from germ. And free sleep. Nothing is birthed in birth that isn't birthed on a berth. Non-birth for the non-syllable. And he's standing there simply'n talking to the wind. Naked and no answer to hone on his logical bone. Or giltbillow fish in an arch and a-leap. Quicksilver! No silver! And butterflies white in the whistling wind. Her mouth in a snarespiring. Oscillating box. Incarnote and spoken. From the grain the sun gets oxygen transfusions. It knocks on the panes of all your museums. Oh mama have I still got my little strawberries? My two penny boo-boos? Mama bent over at the moment. And smiling at him making a hellofafuss. And next to them lighted a whip-full into the face to facing the vertical of the giving given, the gimme, the pipe natura naturans naturata unthought and unclogged. Oh blind prepissings! It's something that's there, and there, and there, and there, and there-there. Strangletheneckofit. Plugupthecuntwithit. Oh mammomicrobes! In a beautiful robe. And the tail of velvet. Of the hooded vulture. Come and be viewed. Verify my vision. It pendulerects rampant to me. And give me a hug. Don't tell papa. Some day you'll have one. Several times bigger. Now nightnight. Consider your miltmilk, nearby the drain redrains in black it's been promised in your hornivory. You'll get out of it and into the shattering curliness, my mummysleketon, my nice mymory. Show me your baby toofy! Little handy touch me! My fleshasaskewer, precious shishkebob! My phial'send! My antler'stem! Mad enbuttedpine! Oh ammine! Ammine!

flight-winging snap veerings pigeons from façades. Wazbad! Spirewind! Generation initially assuming father-form, mother-form, that from son to mother strives to the fore. Grandfather broods over it. He cooking his kettle roiling cover gruel dawns' wheels steamengine beyond water thermodynamic ice with seeds fruit lungs time's rotations. And micro thunderings of orgy-eggings-on. Quotidian procurement. Gorging ration consumption repairing lobby intellect plus necrophiction of its turd scraped-up against the current trash world-conception heightened molding. Every thinker lives at the expense of the singer who hears. Every category is stupefied by connections it reveres. Every priest is struck in doubt-paunch by fears. My child, quoth the old-becassocked codger, today we would be married. The game is up, period. Even our muvvers don't luv us no more. The popy gets nervous and uppilesabull. *That* we want to see. The cunfassanal has ceased to satisfy. Up front's up front, and behind, behind. Abbé boobs' abérrations are all through. Listen. We've held out 2000 years. Ergo, it's all over the place. Kumm flows in ribbers. Ciborium dribbers! I told you when you was little that swell tail about the vergile mary? That tube with no hair settling down so nice and dropping off its creamy load of chrism right by her blubbery heart (lardamus te)? You little slob, you didn't believe it? Did you smell it under their reverend skirts? A fuzzy scent? A rancid clergycandle order? Did you get it? That's our boy! The general is going to feel out the russians. There's also american investment. In asia— give me a minute—it's more complicated. The way they poutout! Inscrewtable! Strumming they've got *real* technique! We're going to have an all-out adultery campaign. I mean honesttogod, transcended, intersected! Ecumenalized! And then: a shiver rumbles. Panchrist panpan. The god Pan alive in our sachristans! Let's go after the leetle gurls! Rend'm 'n blend'm! Orthodox gives us a course on it. *He* knows something about it, measured tone. Unction! Cadences, my child, roarings. They go curazy over it. *Any*thing. Slobber over it! What's more, gluttonish. Reddists. We're going to have our cardfile and our computerre. Perinhenceforward ac penismammary. Shock jezzies. Ad majorem gloriam debabee. We've got a good contact. Tactfully, tactfully. The party all right they need order. Not easy-going, but open, direct, quite potable. Quite findoutable, once you get under their redoubtable! Ah the anguish of the human, my son! We'll try temptation on them. But gently, smirkings. The rest? Same routine. Intrigued for centuries, victims of melo-snobbery. Business is picking up. Don't forget. 2000 years! Restraint, and to a sublime degree! Not one of them who ever did it. It's enough to drive you to. *Nice* people. Open-minded, open-minded, men of good will. Moral, sincere, somewhat common, but what the hell. The planet is well worth a mass. Science is science. The science of living together. Progress is progress. The end justifies the ends. And we've got our means. And grace is, after all, grace. Plus cash, obviously, and *that* we have. Bankaccountedfor, everywhere! From netherlands to alsace-lorraine, from germany all the way to spain, the holyghost from coast to coast! My child, the hour has come: for a generalized (p)ass(toral)-kissing. It's better than acid! Stabler! Sociable! Females: pro! The essencial one! Secure pro eva! Et resurrexit tertia die! Et unam sanctam patholicam ecclesiam! Massive emergency. It's either china or us. De yellowed or us. The Peril! For Croesus! And for the superjeessus! Wretched chinegooks! Atheists, hell-bent! No respect for anything! Don't even attack! Now your russians, you know they *want* something, especially joseph, he's like one of us, basically, male-volent, substantial! But mao! The way he looks! Inhuman! Not even one crime! Not a trace of hell! You know what war is: male-faction for male-faction. With *them* we know what we're dealing with and even make a profit. But china? And note that we've seen it coming from far off! Not for not having thought about it from juzzy to juzzy ex ploiting the puzzy! Rome didn't abet it. Unappily regret it. Faithless adam! And we bust our ash 'n fruitslessly. Machincahoots—let's be! For us, the hitch is finding the sub-itch. And overpopula. The underdeveloped enveloped. Per feminae. Little jesus babymakerprophet. Strategic all-new cure-all curate. Getting right into production! Right into bed with a skip. Heart-lifting dove! Just a sip. For some people, a horizontal father, god in history. Evolution? Aplenty. Ovulation? O ovulationists of every nation, pill it to us! For others, the occult. Funds in reserve! Treasures! Adduced, they adore. Spiritomagism life after death and parapsychism and phantomincorporate! Laughable! All set to go! They'll buy anything! With or without grass! With or without instant wafer! Idyllic trip! Ultralegal joint! Orient of our dreams! Sursum corda! Benedictus qui venit in nomine bambini! The psyche psyched-out! Fast-gaited and eighted! It's ours, the psycha, the downunder pulsars! A private train! In principio erat verbum. Signifikantum! Vroom vroom: boat, we're ready to go! Maximo deo!

and splash mass-angle rapidness expansion collapse of ultra viola dust startangles red infra rising-up con stella. And bang in the lightyear 2000 years before the exclamation hurled in the midst of it returns. Comrade, says globar, we've got to be prudent and patient. There's no proof that you're right. I'm even convinced the contrary is true. We lost our family spirit too soon. We've got to consolidate it by default. I've got no confidence in these chinese. The silence of these non-finite spaces afrights. I'm not a priori against, you know I'm a liberal, but a fortiori I am.

I'm for humility. Besides it's all beyond me. You too. And basically everybody. I believe what I see, I can touch what I've got. What's said is said, and, generally, it's well said. A high and mighty tone offends. Unless the party recommends. In which case, it's said it well because it was what said it. A cat isn't a rat, a rat isn't a cat. Why are you concerned? You'll be overturned. You'll be gristle crushed! You gonna have a real base in your butt, a meta bottom! So you think you're just fine? While you step out of line? And the hierarchy? And modesty? If heads split, I spit! To the party, no opposition! My position: as father of the working classes: I'm pregnant with pride! Warm and cozy inside. If he isn't in me, he's an addled adder. A megalomaniac that thinks he can be he. Our self: reduce it, renounce it, refuse it, repeat it. I am proceedings without subject. A subject that thinks it's proceeding's a slap in the face. I embrace the base. As a basic maso. No mao, *maso*. In social existence men's thought is grounded. Now since I continually approve my social existence, my thought's safe and sounded. I can inthink it, of course. And *you'll* think it by force. China: hide it, lest I be spied. Inside the dark, I was too frightened. Sever us never. Arms around us, harm's groundless. Nurse-maids forever. O france I am with thee! O unifratersity in adversity: let's fight for our rights! I'm sorry but the teacher never talked about the chinese. He's a man who was pure and upright. Sometimes at night—I liked him and we each other—'neath the lamp . . . Against the bourgeois. Against the bourgeois means good en soi. So who proves to me the bourgeoisie don't like the chinese? We've got no proof of it. Nor anybody. That's why I'm against. Radically. Dispassionately. Besides they told me so. Somebody told somebody who told it to me. And I pass it on with a clear conscience. No wool over my eyes. No cathays in our tricksy ways. All for reform. Mum's the word. And no schism in the catechism. China isn't on our route. And that's a cheeseworth of lesson, no doubt. We are the granite of integrity! The salt inturred! Papa said it, mama knew it. Beyond the pyrenees, no way! Maintain the vosges like macho gauls. A gaul's no chinese, no chinese a gaul, that's all I know and all I'll have to know.

gentlemen, the vp says, the situation is not good. Business is merely marking time, with leakings everywhere. The bank is sunk, property run to the ground, the exchange is just what you know. The more we risk on it the more it devours. The 'change is all wet so often that in the end it's mud. Let's inflate prices and loosen our grasp. The unions are aftcr us, reasonable at the top but sometimes, alas, overflowing. Overflowing's the word, but I hope each of you knows how to shore up your banks. Sanctions to begin with. The crisis comes of course from the gold standard. The general's mind was unsound. A kind of tremens. With these histories of history, that's where we're headed. Note, the dollar's still solid. Taking into account that the russians still have stockpiles, by encompassing the announced evolution, it's not impossible that we could re-enroll in the technical transfer to the heart of the pie. Let's lighten the load, eastly does it, aid restoration, industrialize, not fall into a panic. Europe is coming towards us. Socialism should be ours. We'll patch up socialism. Russians very open, but distrust them. Impatient to manage us in their turn. Chinese backward. Let's grab a paddle and make a real mess. Let's dose the kraut the jap with vitamins. The interior in order, the leftist oar-cudgeled with approbation decent people depressed, the police with us especially, not excessively. Don't accelerate on liberties. I want an absolutely clear telly, like bromide itself. Don't forget that the general got screwed because he'd been seen there too much. Shithead plays, shithead games, shit allover. Visual ass-wiping in all. Let's channelize and orientate. Perrault's fables for example. Peter and his pumpkin. The pied piper and publicity. Phony debates false windows, calculated symmetry. And if that rabble gets together, smash it apart, unless of course we stage a revolt. Gentlemen, the situation is not so bad. Barcly two or three incidents. The left, realistic, is taken care of. Money's in a decline, but not vomiting. Order those files. Pursue the cure. Till we meet soon in africa, at the safariclub? Come see my latest painting. My dear, it's an exquisite rose color, salmon, I put it into the little desk, on the right. My wife is re-reading proust. As for me, I don't give a damn about writers. My wife and her psychia, it's all very touchy. But, dear, you know mine's signed up, by god! No? Yes she is! For real! Solemn conversion! Revergin! I thought she was on the left? Once! Not long ago! A little! Now, let's get back to business! Unionized! Arranged! More travel! Morning, dupont, hold the market steady. Car! Car! Get ready! Here we go into the flow!

modern revisionists defend critical realism with so much zeal because they're also the spokesmen for the decadent bourgeoisie. Unsurpassable form, they say, my ass. Embellishing by exploiters, workers peasants presented as hooligans flunkeys, history in reverse, theory of egoism, aestheticism, birdshit. Renaissance, century of enlightenment, without exception they fit back into the framework of classical bourgeois literature and art. Love art in yourselves, they say, meaning assured capital fame. Theory of germs, double nature. Human essence heaven-fallen innate without application the same for everybody, bull. So-called ideas coming from the brain like bile social aspect of the question lost and erased for good reason. Infantile representation history made by heroes saints prophets the masses absent which the true hero on the other hand reflects and comprehends. A priorism conservative ultra-liberal rupture between subjective objective confusion existence conscience cult origin so-called self-education negation of the masses. All of it evolving towards class-reconciliation passivity hazy entity patriarchy redecorated fat butts knowledge cut off from practical application again spectral psyche half-concealing its myths. But we've got to unite politics and truth. Bring forward as evidence contradictions conflicts, not repeated isolated events. Revolutionary realism romanticism innovation originality limits of the individual aspiring infinite social relationships emerging chaos. Leaving sugared abstraction contemplation of the same lilines entering black torrent for bloodying two prolo hands. It's of advantage to the writer who's dying of boredom to repeat his little performances till night-night. At the end of his ten-thousandth sentence on despair vague sensation dream clothespins and sex-purrings amid widespread yawns, he sees clearly the phantasm impasse. Enough's enough superfluous characters allusions always useless reflections of what of whom why how I ask you it doesn't know anything and pretends to at the drop of a hat. While real actors have two minutes to piss in the washrooms. Up yours. Shut up. Bonuses hammered drum bigshots kingpins and cops if there's one word out of line. Watch out for your fingers. Pointing metronome carriage afar desks decoys glossy paper liver-complaint. Typists devastated click click in the computaclick fatigue packer ditto sweeper ditto machinist and welder and cutter and smelter. Under glass casings steel framework vast sound. Hand me the tract. Condense all that while we group for the attack. Analyze. Draft. In a word or two. And do you recall the flash visit of the revisionist popoet who came to encourage us in the name of his mill in the country and his suntan lamp? And in addition we'd have to repeat it seems his garglings, his verse as they say. The dirty mothers. Rotten collabos. Worse than the bourgeois. Similar shittier senile paternalism moist palm on buttocks dribbling on himself like an idiot. Poet take up your viol! For class violence. And to hell with everything else! And not one bribe, from the depths of the coma! And on all fronts, with whoever wants to! And cultivate yourself. Study philo, you can use it. Spotting instinctively what they don't like. It seems the chinese have got a grudge? That they've eliminated drudgery, like it or lump it? And that they're numerous on their tabula rasa? The bigshots are against, but it's coming along, it's getting through, whoever lives will see. In spite of censure and club me on the head. Whatever's growing down there has everything in front of it. Whoever sees will live and remember

students, don't let them grind you down. Now's no time for sitting. Revival, they call it—just the crazy old dream. Empiricofadiddled for fillyassoffy. Criticize, criticize, there'll still be something left. Ask to see the books. Nice and clear, for the crooks. Record and classify their balledphrased lies. Look at their eyes. Reeducatize. Set up plans for study. Don't buy their cruddy junk. Never debunk—be right with the party—the fight. Opium is the religion of the anti-people. Revisionism is the most antipopular form of opium. The bourgeois and the revisiono, hand in glove, in an elliptic concerted devious evolution, will shaft you. Fight back, counterattack. Disorder contains and intensifies order, mad as hatterers, the way they turn on to flatterers. The policified-anarcho's got to go. Not a bad guy, nice, but short on brains, you know. Spitting isn't splitting. Getting high's not getting through. Crashing down a closed door doesn't guarantee it stays open. And so: to arms! Study their weak points. If you haven't got theory, it's just screwing around. Take everything at face value. Psychia, first off, obviously, is something very organed. Keep an eye on it. Dialectics can be learned. And practiced. Unpracticed it's only a pilacrap. Study history. It'll get you farther. A garbage can, even an historic one, is no good for eliminating a lapsed philosophy. Putting a philosophy out with the trash is a hundred times more efficient than putting out, stricto sensu, a philosophy teacher. A teacher in the trash can can breed ten more trashcans that think they can teach. You can see it already. If your right hand takes dope, your left hand doesn't have to know. Metaphysics actually consists in bringing your hands together. Support women who don't want to fuse into one any longer. No need to get mad—just say I've had it! Subjective preparation is necessary. Which doesn't mean subjectivism, sectarianism. They come too often from your stereotyped style. Too many of our comrades currently involved in propaganda haven't learned the language. So their propaganda is boring and not many people enjoy reading their articles or hearing their speeches. Put an end to empty and endless orations. Intimidating isn't persuading. The saying about playing a lute for an ox implies scorn for the audience. But look at it the other way and the scorn hits the player. Don't force yourself to speak or write, if you haven't got anything to say. Because if you don't, you won't be able to criticize somebody who has something to say to the point. The true gets strong in its struggle with the false. But not by boxing its ears. Which means that the false gets strong too and you've got to give it credit. What's more, the false is deaf. Marxism is a scientific truth. It's not afraid of criticism and doesn't get beaten down. If you don't get all of this, and, even worse, if you don't understand it at all, you're apt to make the most serious mistakes and not appreciate the necessity for struggle on the ideological level. And from that point on, shtuff, revisiono-applause, sucker, on the spot. Your style should be more alive, fresher. More vivid, more popular. Don't just say proletariat! proletariat! Ask yourself what *they'd* say if they were you. Don't lose your cool if your teachers look sarcastic. They're over-refined; just leave them behind. They always know less than you think. Say what they say but more clearly. And you can turn it around, right in front of them. Humor is your weapon, your surrational. Give up surrealism that only nourishes subrealism; the two of them, along with the so-called "natural," have got a dubious stench of urinals and churches. Be affirmative. Running isn't enough: you've got to brake in time. Get through the porno-stage, with self-observation. Watch out for people who always write the same sentences. Their musicless hearts are as black as erebus. While I'm at it, let me say to the reader who hasn't gotten this far that he's made a big mistake. I don't approve his pollution all *that* much. Mistake, I say, because only the tie-up gnawing sedimentation relaxation of inhibition can, degree by degree, prove the sense, can circumstance my inadance.

—trans. William H. Matheson and Emma Kafalenos

Helmut Heissenbüttel

contrat social

someone is with someone else and let's assume they are the only ones there one
is this way and the other isn't either the one will become half not this way and
the other half this way or they'll try to separate or one will kill the other or the
other the one and everything is done

but now there are three and let's still assume they are the only ones there one is
this way and the second too and the third isn't or one is this way and the second
and third aren't etc. now either one will become half this way and the other two
half not this way or the other way round or they'll all become neither nor this
way etc. or they'll try to separate or two will kill the third or one the other two
and everything is done

but now there are four or five or fifty or a thousand or one hundred thousand or a
million or two and a half billions and everyone is different from the others many
not very different but all a little bit many of course are also a bit similar and because again and again there are some that are a bit similar they get along and
there isn't killing and murder all the time to the extent that no one would be left
but those who get along because of the little bit they have in common are now
already somewhat more different from those who get along because of another
little bit they have in common

and if they don't find still another something which they have a little bit in common with the others things go wrong and indeed there is killing and murder aggression and defense Blitzkrieg saturation bombing invasion and surrender and
nevertheless nothing is done

but finally several many who are a little bit similar and get along find a little something they have in common with other many who are a little bit similar and again other many find again other many and now there are on one side the several many who are first a little bit and then still another little bit of a bit and finally a little bit of a little little bit similar and get along and on the other side the other several many who have another little bit and still another little bit of a bit and finally still another little bit of another little bit a little bit in common and get along and let's assume they are the only ones there two and a half billion roughly then they form two blocks and cannot get along even if they all knew Esperanto

210

—trans. Rosmarie Waldrop

Apartheid

we can accomplish much perhaps everything except the one thing getting to the other side we are sentenced for good to staying on this side and those who are over there might even mistake it for a privilege that we are sentenced to this but we don't

we like to imagine that there must have been a time once when the choice hadn't been made yet everything was still undivided mixed as it were a time beyond guilt and hope

but we only imagine this because we can't stop wishing to reduce the decided decision to something perhaps still decidable

the fact that we are sentenced to staying on this side has nothing to do with pre-destination and decidability because there was no time of decidability and the only choice that between repugnance and assent

even if someone which was impossible could have gotten to the other side it wouldn't have abolished the sides and we who are sentenced to staying on this side can't even speak as if we spoke from the other side because our speech is waterproof as it were with this side and not even reason helps us across

even though we disavow what happened or deny that what we helped establish will continue our disavowals and our denials undeniably prove only one thing that we are sentenced to staying on this side sentenced the more irrevocably the more our disavowals and our denials seem to contradict themselves and the most we can accomplish is a response to this contradiction as to a platform hesitantly raised in no-man's-land where perhaps some of us can meet some of you but no more

and even if we in spite of everything think looking backward that there were single occasions when we could have gotten over to your side the mere memory that it could only have been us who would have gone proves that it can't have been a matter of occasions but only again of wishful thinking fallacies of guilt inspired by no longer curable guilt feelings

212

perhaps after an infinite time we will succeed in coming closer if only infinitely little closer to you without your recoiling from us which nobody would blame you for least of all we perhaps we would succeed during this infinite time in coming so infinitely close to you that you could nearly no longer speak of this side and the other side

in a certain sense this is the only hope of our only reserved contradiction on this side

—trans. Rosmarie Waldrop

New Era

when who meets whom and what he says when who runs into whom and then he
says what when who calls whom what

when a cold warrior meets a cold warrior and says cold warrior when a fellow
traveler meets a fellow traveler and says fellow traveler when an old nazi calls an
old nazi an old nazi

when an intellectual calls an intellectual an old nazi when an avantgardist meets
an avantgardist and says cold warrior when a nonconformist meets a nonconformist and says fellow traveler

when a fellow traveler meets a fellow traveler and says half pint hood when an
old nazi calls an old nazi an experimentalist when a cold warrior meets a cold
warrior and says queer bastard

when an intellectual meets an old nazi and says queer bastard when an avantgardist calls a cold warrior an experimentalist when a nonconformist meets a fellow traveler and says half pint hood

when a half pint hood meets a half pint hood and says old nazi when an experimentalist meets an experimentalist and says fellow traveler when a queer bastard
calls a queer bastard an intellectual

when he calls him that when he meets him and then says that when he runs into
him and says that then

everybody joins the communist party and lives happily ever after

  —trans. Rosmarie Waldrop

The Future of Socialism

nobody owns anything
nobody exploits
nobody oppresses
nobody is exploited
nobody is oppressed
nobody wins anything
nobody loses anything
nobody is master
nobody is slave
nobody is superior
nobody is subordinate
nobody owes anything to you
nobody does anything to you

nobody owns nothing
nobody exploits nobody
nobody oppresses nobody
nobody is exploited by nobody
nobody is oppressed by nobody
nobody wins nothing
nobody loses nothing
nobody is master of nobody
nobody is slave of nobody
nobody is superior to nobody
nobody is subordinate to nobody
nobody owes anything to nobody
nobody does anything to nobody

everybody owns everything
everybody exploits everybody
everybody oppresses everybody
everybody is exploited by everybody
everybody is oppressed by everybody
everybody wins everything
everybody loses everything
everybody is master of everybody
everybody is slave of everybody
everybody is superior to everybody
everybody is subordinate to everybody
everybody owes everything to everybody
everybody does everything to everybody

everybody owns nothing
everybody exploits nobody
everybody oppresses nobody
everybody is exploited by nobody
everybody is oppressed by nobody
everybody wins nothing
everybody loses nothing
everybody is master of nobody
everybody is slave to nobody
everybody is subordinate to nobody
everybody owes nothing to nobody
everybody does nothing to nobody

   —trans. Rosmarie Waldrop

Gerhard Rühm

```
          unite                        unite
           unite                      unite
            unite                    unite
             unite                  unite
              unite                unite
               unite              unite
                unite            unite
                 unite          unite
                  unite        unite
                   unite      unite
                    unite    unite
                     unite  unite
                      unitunite
                      ununite
                       unite
```

Lucia Marcucci

Il Tema romantico della poesia

17

Politics and the Avant-Garde

The political irony and self-parody of many avant-garde texts reveal how this movement of aesthetic activism is divided against itself. Historically, the avant-garde has been socially progressive but unsure about the specific relationship of artistic action to social praxis. Unquestionably, the avant-garde is the product of bourgeois society, created by bourgeois writers and artists and sustained by the bourgeois cultural institutions it calls into question. Thus, its aggressive behavior necessarily undermines the avant-garde's belief that it is a revolutionary force in its culture if it fails to recognize its class situation. And even contemporary writers like Sollers, who incorporate Marxist thinking into their social and aesthetic vision, often find themselves alienated from traditional Marxist ideology; they find themselves placing more faith in radical thinkers and artists like themselves than in the masses that Marxists maintain will be the primary agents of real social change.

Amiri Baraka, who has written some of the most innovative and powerful plays, fiction, and poetry, in his recent work offers a strong critique of avant-garde writers caught within the dilemmas of modernist and postmodernist self-consciousness. These idealist writers—skymen—may find a semblance of personal freedom in the skies of formal invention, but they are awkward and confused when on the earth of actual social conditions. These grounded skymen are no Baudelairian albatrosses of the imagination. There is no post-romantic nostalgia for the infinite here. Baraka insists that the poet write to and among the people, speaking not of individualistic anxieties, but of collective needs and potentiality. Baraka's poetry finds its innovative style, its language and rhythm in the streets. The imagery he uses is simple and direct.

Simple and direct also are the works of Paul de Vree, whose visual poems combine images and words of depersonalization, pain, and violence with brutal economy.

Amiri Baraka

A Poem for Deep Thinkers

Skymen coming down out the clouds land
and then walking into society try to find out
whats happening—"Whats happening," they be saying
look at it, where they been, dabbling in mist, appearing &
disappearing, now there's a real world breathing—inhaling exhaling
concrete & sand, and they want to know what's happening. What's happening
is life itself "onward & upward," the spirals of fireconflict clash
of opposing forces, the dialogue of yes and no, showed itself in stabbed children
in the hallways of schools, old men strangling bankguards, a hard puertorican
    inmate's tears
exchanging goodbyes in the prison doorway, armies sweeping wave after wave
    to contest
the ancient rule of the minority. What draws them down, their blood entangled
    with humans,
their memories, perhaps, of the earth, and what they thought it could be. But
    blinded by
sun, and their own images of things, rather than things as they actually are,
    they wobble,
they stumble, sometimes, and people they be cheering alot, cause they think
    the skymen
dancing, "Yeh . . . Yeh . . . get on it . . . ," people grinning and feeling good
    cause the skymen
dancing, and the skymen stumbling, till they get the sun out they eyes, and
    integrate the
inhead movie show, with the material reality that exists with and without
    them. There are

tragedies tho, a buncha skies bought the loopdieloop program from the elegant babble of

the ancient minorities. Which is where they loopdieloop in the sky right on just loopdieloop

in fantastic meaningless curlicues which delight the thin gallery owners who wave at them

on their way to getting stabbed in the front seats of their silver alfa romeos by lumpen

they have gotten passionate with. And the loopdieloopers go on, sometimes spelling out

complex primitive slogans and shooting symbolic smoke out their gills in honor of something

dead. And then they'll make daring dives right down toward the earth and skag cocaine money

whiteout and crunch iced into the statue graveyard where Ralph Ellison sits biting his banjo

strings retightening his instrument for the millionth time before playing the star spangled

banjo. Or else loopdieloop loopdieloop up higher and higher and thinner and thinner and finer

refiner, sugarladdies in the last days of the locust, sucking they greek lolliepops.

Such intellectuals as we is baby, we need to deal in the real world, and be be in the real

world. We need to use, to use, all the all the skills all the spills and thrills that we

conjure, that we construct, that we lay out and put together, to create life as beautiful

as we thought it could be, as we dreamed it could be, as we desired it to be, as we knew it

could be, before we took off, before we split for the sky side, not to settle for endless

meaningless circles of celbration of this madness, this madness, not to settle for this

madness this madness madness, these yoyos yoyos of the ancient minorities. Its
    all for real,
everything's for real, be for real, song of the skytribe walking the earth, faint
    smiles to
open roars of joy, meet you on the battlefield they say, they be humming, hop,
    then stride,
faint smile to roars of open joy, hey my man, what's happening, meet you on
    the battlefield
they say, meet you on the battlefield they say, what i guess needs to be
    discussed here tonight
is what side yall gon be on

Like—This Is What I Meant!

Poetry makes a statement
            like everything
            like everything poetry
            makes a statement
Poetry is a being of words
        a being of language flicks
        produced by the life
        of   (DAH DAAAAAA!!)
    "ThE pOeT"
But here is where we differ
from Funk & Wagnalls, Empson
        Thaddeus Dustface
        & the rest of assorted bourgeois functionaries
        of the inherited
            decaying
            superstructure

"Take Class Struggle
        as the Key Link," sd Mao, "Act according
                    to principles
                    laid
                    down."

So that even in our verse
The roar of raging mass
is heard

So that
even in our
        verse
                the struggle
                erupts, the 4 fundamental contradictions
                in the world
                today
                Leap out in
                relief,

                So that even
                in our verse
                we move by vibrations with the unstoppable
                masses, advancing
                the
                Chairman sd,
                "Wave upon
                Wave,"
                So that even
                in our verse, we are transported
                by the billion voiced mass
                chanting revolutionary slogans
                as they sweep forward to
                                crush
                                the piss faced
                                bourgeoisie

                "Countries want Independence
                Nations want Liberation
                People want Revolution," Chairman Mao
                                        has sd
                                        & we act
                                        according
                                        to principles
                                        laid down.

Poetry must sing, laugh & fight
Poetry must reveal, probe and light
Poetry must take class struggle
             as the key link
             must remould its world view
             to take up the struggle
             for the mighty
             working
             class

Poetry must see as its central task
             building
         a Marxist-Leninist
             Communist Party
             in the USA

So that even in our verse
we wage ideological struggle over political
line
engage in struggle
guided by M-L-M

to get a program for a party
and a party for our
program
So that
even in
our verse
our song

we are working for
the change
no,
      this aint strange

So that even
even in our verse,   our poetry
                 our song
     we are building human
                explosion

     to smash
     capitalism
     to smash
     to smash
     capitalism
     to smash
     to smash
     capitalism

So that even in our verse
the irresistible tide of revolution
is unleashed
yes
unleashed

So that even
   in our verse
this Red Explosion
   is unleashed

Yeh
unleashed

So that even
  in our
  verse
  even in
  our dancing
  even in
  our song
  yeh
  in our pure lover song

  REVOLUTION!!!

Paul de Vree

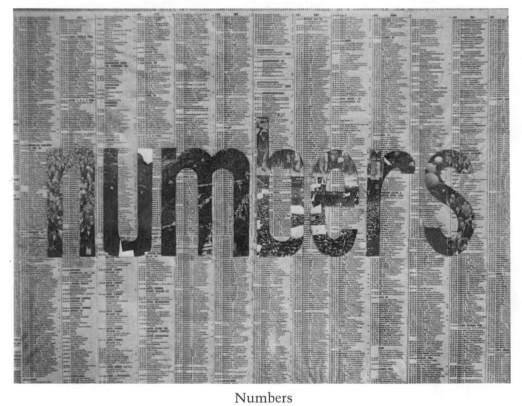

Numbers

Anniversary Date of Rubens

Nothing Has Changed

The Street Tells the Truth

Notting Hill

18
Political Ambivalence of the Avant-Garde

Baraka's work is grounded in the assurance that pre-revolutionary conditions exist in this society, and that all one's activities, including literary creation, can and should be shaped and propelled by the forces of imminent change. Thus, even though an individual writer may disrupt reigning literary conventions, his or her innovations are to be seen not as expressions of an individualistic sensibility seeking purely personal articulation and gratification, but as embodiments of a collective movement.

However, most avant-garde writers today—as well as radical post-structuralist critics and revisionist Marxist theorists—despair of the revolutionary potential of the working class. Workers seem to have been successfully incorporated into the modern organizational capitalist state. Instead, these writers remain committed to a literary and intellectual tradition, perhaps more prone to seek evidence of the continued existence of oppositional, or negative, thinking than to look for signs of immediate material change. In this context, the avant-garde's self-reflexive approach to language and social codes of meaning and behavior represents an expression of that search, even as it suggests a possible model of behavioral and conceptual radicalism. The spirit of play and freedom—the apparently gratuitous moment born of disruption and self-reflexive creation—intimates the possibility of a new model of action and being, a new dream of personal and collective freedom.

Nevertheless, each step toward a new aesthetic and ethic is labored and tentative because the goals demand an acceptance of incomplete or temporary identity, partial self-control, limited articulation, and irrational or disruptive vision. Throughout each experiment in literary discourse, each exploration of the social text, the doubt, paranoia, and overbearing sense of vulnerability that mark the personal context can be felt. The personal and social realms collapse into each other and the face of the future often looks bleak, even to these writers willfully in advance of their time.

The setting of Severo Sarduy's *Maitreya* is a world in flux, specifically the Near and Far East, once under the shadow of the West but now emerging into their own power and vision. That emergence, however, takes the form of a grotesque ritual in which characters now cut off from their own past submit to sadomasochistic parodies of the world they resent and envy. Over all, Lady Tremendous reigns, putative incarnation of some future Buddha, a figure against whom those who abuse themselves are judged.

Maurice Roche's work bears all the distinguishing marks of recent avant-garde innovation—fragmentation of character, narrative, and language; self-reflexive structural and linguistic play; social rebellion and personal self-creation. It also reaches no satisfying resolution concerning the tensions among personal, aesthetic, and social contexts. In *CodeX*, for example, the narrative voice is obsessed from its very beginnings with forced endings. Here, in two sections from the book (which include the last pages), the fear of death, of the self, of language, and of society that dominates the work culminates in apocalypse. As in Sollers's novel, the text confronts its own language and author, and specifically the conflicts of writing and being written. In addition, it attempts to define itself and its world, while finding itself defined by its language and social ideology instead. Rather than demonstrating a faith in mastering language and the text, Roche's work reveals a process in which desire discovers itself prey to manipulation. Self-creation is doomed by natural decay, and the social domain is subject to sinister control.

Throughout the novel, from behind the text, intimations of silence and death in the image of a skull appear—here, in the very cries for peace. Everything seems necessarily propelled toward personal and collective death, while the speakers, the characters, the writer, and society all do their best to deny it.

Severo Sarduy

From *Maitreya*

"The Fist"

Hurling zeros and suras, swiftly brushing past other Mercedes, they cross the city. The concave front windows reflect, with excessive clarity, passersby, trees, store windows—neon Arabic letters, fig boxes—fleeing toward the windshield that duplicates the opposite sidewalk: a man in shirt and tie who looks to the right, squinting his eyes, and on the yellow stripes of the pavement an old man in a white beard is about to rest his heel. Dome in the distance, brick minarets, cluster of loudspeakers.

They—who?—: Lady Tremendous, goddess or queen, ibis or kiss; the dwarf, and a local cat, disguised as Emirs from the Persian Gulf, in Moorish cloaks, black braids around their foreheads, English accents and green sunglasses. And then there's the chauffeur: lowered to fucker-by-the-hour who, to revenge the duo's tortuosities, sets free the back seat amplifiers: a vile and Andaloose music drills the right eardrum and mini-labyrinth of the left. They bite their hides, beg for earplugs, swallow furious lysergical raspberries:

"To the desert, to the desert," they rant and rave, adamant. Through the scanty windows framed by the slabs of that blue then copied by the Chinese, one could see, beyond the red minarets, the snowy mountains. On the tile floor, in tin washbowls and polished pitchers, a dense and creamy water settled, with which the dwarf rubbed the clients. From the bones of the feet, which he stretched one by one till they cracked, to the scalp, the brief assistant greased the gentlemen with that ointment. In a gray felt hat like a helmet, he came in and out, drawing open an opaque curtain; he couldn't manage with the pails: his arms trembled.

Fed up with boredom and petrodollars, the turbaned magnates ran from the ever-inflamed towers—and even some, emerald yokes, from Maracaibo—rosaries of big amber beads, Koran in hand.

Stretched out among prophylactic vapors, on a fringed tapestry of nomad motifs, Lady Tremendous underwent the apotheosis of the fist. She divided infinitely divisible branches, she censured, for their impurities, other contacts. She was surrounded by the chauffeur and his old buddies, persistent like her, big mustachioed machos with big bellies, shirts and flies opened. They were having bloody marys.

A galaxy of lightbulbs yellowed the small living room. Among piles of rolled tapestries the binary initiates left their bicycles. In the next chamber gifts accumulated: wrought dishes, lamps, candelabra, hookahs, a mannerist Toledan apostle, and a portrait of Kennedy, in canvas and bas-relief. After making their offerings, they'd go up a spiral staircase until disappearing into the soffit of stalactites, among burnt flags. They'd order yoghurt with effervescent water. They'd go out drunk into the street. The wind was blowing so that it drove you crazy.

They catechized among scaffolds, in the ruins of a mosque. Among the riggings which supported the dome, pigeons nested. Thirsty silk merchants arrived in caravans. The wind raised red sand, frozen drops.

A hawk perched on her forefinger, the wealthy and robust Lady Tremendous widened her pupils, arched her eyebrows, looked to the left to indicate "forbidden." The dwarf dragged himself convulsively to her feet, screaming like a newborn rabbit being devoured by a red-haired dog. They ate dried fruit.

The faithful swiftly crossed the patio. A big eye. Covered in black rags. Reflected in one another, quartered polygons formed blue buildings, walls which decomposed into other walls, rotating domes, palm trees.

From a marble serving dish with geometric designs—the name of the prophet, stylized—Lady Tremendous scooped out with a big spoon thick glazed syrup with lumps of caramel and sugar candy, which she served to the initiates. The potion started putting them to sleep. Sluggishly they circled the Great White Lady. Yes, they adored her for being fat and creamy. Fists raised high, the idolaters asked her to bless the scrofulous and the virulent, to guide disputes or to save lambs. In little blue lamps, the tip crushed by fingers, hemp burned in oil.

In the distance one could see the lights of a toy-filled bazaar. A tomb in the middle of a pool. Carvers of turquoise and white forehead stones labored in nearby porticos.

Back to the baths—there the stereophonic chauffeur awaited them—they gave into the prescribed infamies: in translucent gray nylon baggy trousers, tightened with elastic at the thighs, they played with dirty water. The dwarf, sporting an Austrian midwife's apron and a protruding gold dental plate, brought over, on a metal cart for serving hors d'oeuvres, a douche jug with a fat spout and a Pompeyan nozzle. With solid vaseline and in the presence of the chauffeur and other confused fans—sniffing dirty old men, stinky truck-drivers, masseurs and masturbators—he impaled the Overwhelming Lady, clumsily, with the porcelain prick filled with a gluey water that swelled up inside.

They played with excrement and coins. They drank fermented palm juice. Splattered with urine, they painted black masks.

First he put his joined fingertips into the anus, as if to close a flower or caress the snout of a tapir; then, the hand already inside up to the wrist, he turned it slowly, with precaution, from one side to the other, as if waiting for the slight sound that opens a strong box.

In the tiles Lady Tremendous saw the reflection of the hand sinking in, as if into another body, between her rosy, rather soft, buttocks. Luminous, it went in and out; a thin glove, the lubricant seemed to envelop it like a piston.

Then the chauffeur appeared with an unfolded screen on his head, as if protecting himself from a gale wind. Right in front of the gasping actants, he extended, with false modesty, the tense screen joined by thick hinges. Behind it, he placed on the floor two large lamps.

Through one of the shutters the obese lady was lifting the cloak with her left hand, revealing a neatly formed fleshy knee. The tip of her shoe brushed the fabric. A little hand with its fingers tightly joined, as if in a mallet, appeared before her spread gluteals. At wrist level, it was cut off by the crack.

The expansion of Islam and/or petroleum had unchained in that country, as in many others, an Ayatollesque mania of "seeing everything big." Soon it was deduced, though never uttered, among the megalomaniac businessmen of the steamy establishment, that a talkative and crooked scanty being, planted in the midst of that set of satraps in bloom, was, and don't feel hurt, an intolerable buffoonery to the imperial vanity.

With the rise of the flaming petrodollar, the new breed rushed to the tidy blue tiles of the house of ablutions—reflections of jewels and newly coined dinars crossed the resinous vapors of the sauna—; with the rising class the dissipating dwarf arrived at the perversion of his handlings. In a mutilated pyramidal cap like an Assyrian hunter's, and on his wrists so many trinkets with phrases ciphered like groped and grateful impresarios, he want staggering up the tin stepladder. The plated soles of his orthopedic bootees resounded against the steps, coins falling on an aluminum drum. His little hands reached table level: the stiff customer lay wrapped in a cloth dampened in camphorated oil as if in a greenish shroud. With the remedial fluctuation began the clinking of the offered bracelets and the racket of the nodding stepladder. The ointment of boiled nettles was seasoning beneath the chaste towel the bulky or swollen body.

He reached, and that was his loss, such spare and speedy methods that, now without basis or caution, his hands repeated on their own the prophylactic movements, like a swimmer on dry land. The sassy whore-hopper would crumble onto the couch and, ipso facto, the showy ding-a-ling would resound, without further introduction than the vaselined hand: deepening pleasure, he also deepened without further ado the gloved and shiny embalmed fingers into the loosened sphincters of the despots.

His mannered manipulations contaminated his muffled clientele: there were those who went to be humiliated by an Abyssinian swimmer, a vulgar braggart deliberately contracted by the house, in simulated gymnastic classes.

The mild-mannered stretched awkward bellows between their arms, provoked punching bags, rowed out of rhythm or leaped hydropically upon a cork mattress as the Master sardonically giggled, inviting the eventual knuckle-blows of his pretended irritation.

Behind a thick colored glass door, where the screen of a giant television was reflected, one could imagine the creeps on pedals, obediently imitating the half-naked and oiled leader ready to correct the slightest fault.

Others, more tortuous, required programmed furies: every Tuesday, under the promotional impetus of leather and rock—which the ticket seller, to drown out ays and whip-snappings, turned on full blast—several solvent and mild old men assembled for belt lashings, slaps and burns, with their remunerated chastisers.

"And clic and clac!" the dwarf hummed mockingly, leaping like a grasshopper amid the morbid cubicle.

And, according to the reception of his digital assaults, he continued cataloguing S's and M's for the next session.

—trans. Suzanne Jill Levine

Maurice Roche

From *CodeX*, Section One

Unity of mobile-selinite-dwelling —pretext: in the Empyrean, fragment of the moon colonized by imperialist necessity.

      w h e r e
      everyone
      being (by
      dasein?)

A society useless to insist upon.—*The living in slow motion*, in pressurized straight jackets, fireproofed, isolating as much as possible making them all alike, aseptic, *conditioned by their wrapping, uniform.*

"Underwater City"—inverse, crepuscular world, deaf, mute, slow.

At noon, it's twilight. The paths of light crossing the waters seem to emanate from the abysses as through the stained-glass windows of an ENGULFED CATHEDRAL. The homes, only perceptible by torchlight, are made from steel hulls and are able to withstand pressures of up to 100 lbs. per sq. inch—why not? Seek buried treasure in the wrecks—and seek to conquer and exploit the neighboring domain: the continental shelf—up to the embankment overlooking the domain of the abysses. Endless source of raw materials for future super-industries: crude oil in the first place, titanium, iron, chromium, aluminum, magnesium, potassium, gold, diamonds—drugs:

> Preach the ecstatic intoxication of the great bottom = narcosis anesthetizing reason—and avoid it by wearing incompressible water-tight garments.

Open the era of a new industrial routine
        the profitability of the UNDER WORLD.

Communicate in sign language

Fallout-shelter town.—concave. Modern refuge of the masters

(Survivors united like the five letters/fingers).　　Everything　here

planned for the maintenance of a clear conscience,　e.g. :

forget—in other words:

　　　　　　　　　　　　　　　　　　　　in supreme comfort

be　able　　to contemplate appreciate the residues/treasures of thought,

/of life

　　　　　　　　　　　　　　　　—patrimony in reserve

reserved for the elite

　　　　　　　　　　　　　　　　for example : gathered

in　a　test　tube　(graduated?)　and　conserved　at　−60°F.,　a　bit

of male seed ——————————————— for posterity

　　　　　　　　　　　　　　　　and　　also

—paintings of/for　the　masters,　advertising　posters,　placards,

trophies, objets d'art

Prison camp barbed wire on plaster pedestal: ready-made for exhibit engaged in worldliness

have for free the boss's head on the T.V. screen

243

Impossibility Propensity of confusing the (r)uses **with the exploiters cultivating respect (the traditions) of**

in place interchangeable—irremovable—imposing a high aesthetic level to the horror of the routine scoop, with no information but well presented; the daily containing in depth propaganda confusion, **the human being— conformity, that is! all the time entertaining the good sentiments (for a base) and several gracious small persons (for the form)**

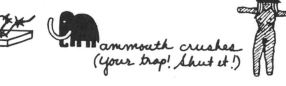 ammouth crushes (your trap! Shut it!) estify

Our Father who art —very watchful

Stylized mammoth crushing prices and workers

244

An Eve (a girl) in a poster—remarkably poised; a dream creature in flesh and apparently in form: a doll "swelled with pride," pin-up proposing a toast to an unforseeable victory

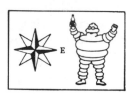

Stop up the wound which is the mouth the adhesive lip-stick ("carefully clean the surfaces to be glued"). Dry instantly and weld forever the kiss of the collage onto the eternal leer of death.

Umgestürzte Zitadelle. Fall-out shelter destined for the people's representatives. Be unaware of it while all the time knowing it.

(Apart from the universe?)

Imagine the subterranean streets, the walls of the corridors papered with advertisements for elections and for peace reproducing peace *(always) out of hand* (positive); . . . politics of the "tendered hand" in back: heavy hands on

STADIUM. DESERT(ED).

City. Miniature.

Resuming. The. History. Of. All. Instruments. Of. Torture. —
Stakes. — Trinkets. Playthings. Gadgets. In. This. Gymnasi-
um. *Showcase.*

Inventions. Testifying. To. The. Creative. Spirit. Distributed.
In. The. Sense. Of. The. Senses. For. Pleasure.

With which to twist the body and give it all of its suppleness in
stiffness Grow thin down to the bone, down to the skeleton by
spatial games first come first starved in a dance macabre

Unbreakable !Thebonesaresetbypressure(don'tglueuptheworks
norsticktoit!Nopastetogo.) Anatomicallyauthentic.Realistical-
lyjointed.

This astonishing model of a human skeleton sits down, stands
up, leans over, walks, takes the most unexpected poses. For doc-
tors, therapists, artists, students, etc. The American techniques
of mass production allowing us to lower the prices. . . .

Depriving man of his movements and operations,

for dea*th*, better there not rendeth it in effigy than
to accompare it to repose—and for the dea*d* to accompany
them to rest by funeral march and requiem.

From *CodeX*, Section Two

Freedom of city

Prototype of Machine Town/floating
/mechanical/ideal/three-dimensional:

That being put—flat (on the paper
evidently), and so that the illusion
is complete, make believe that it is
enough to substitute for a blindfold
re-covering your sight with darkness—three-dimensional glasses.

Re-covering

your vision of this "elect.^ed_ion place"

(see red with the left eye and with
the right nothing, but blue(s)), discover
then an impalpablè "Uncomposed in Space."

**Die Poeten uund Orators vor-
zeiten haben gesagt in iren
Sprüchen** *quando o urubu està
de azar, o urubu de baixo caga
no de cima,* nur keine Angst, Ich
bin Vegetarier! *quando buffiamo
del buon Dio, possiamo inghiottire
qualsiasi cosa* **und Sententzen, das**

Thinking of those who are hungry, let your
tears flow "freely"

Help them to shorten their suffering
by supporting a bond of armaments (!!!)
bombardment
—a special drawing taking place
(more and more) frequently.

die Gedechtnus des Ellends *jan-*
ma–mrtyu–jarâ–duh–kha–(bis)
uund Armuot vorlangst erlitten
ist ain grosser Lust!

Havah nivnè lanou *promettre le ciel*
ir oumigdal berocho bachamayim
THE PHALLUS-SHELL THAT RIDES
THROUGH *a shining vagina of steel*
soars THROUGH THE SKY.

help yourself to others *en breu veir-*
em Fan, farelerelan, fan *fields lit-*
tered with quarters they are confused they are lost, all is . . . *and of*
fendutz ferlore la tintelore . . . *per*
bustz tro als braiers all is ferlore, bei
Gott!

BOOM

Raise very high—fix the price there

Explain that a loan (or a collection)
    allows one to simultaneously lower
    taxes and control unemployment by
    introducing *fine*, new money

Encourage the poor of rich countries to
    give their last red cent to the rich
    of underdeveloped countries, thus
       overexposed
    helping to maintain a certain
    balance of power

in presence

                             of delegates
at the lecture, at the conference,
at the seminary (what a word!) at

the symposium, at the congress for the
congratulation of highnesses and other
upstarts

The aim of the one who has some bread being to have you acquit him (!?)

For the creation of things
in the sole perspective of
their disappearance,

it is ordered:
"Cross and multiply—thus
everything will be consumed!"

it is proposed:
"Badly paid of the *world*,
indict : be **continent**"

A lowering of salaries *gheest my
wyt bermherticheyt* being priceless
yet waer un ie ghevoed magh zunch

We shall maintain peace **Vergel-
tungswaffen** even though we must
go to war for it! AND THEN IGNITES
INTO THE EARTH

τῆλε μὰλ ἧχι βάθιστον ὑπὸ χθονὸς ἐστι βέρεθρον·

TO ward and against everything
man Protected Prohibited

"or techniques and future sciences of developing. . . ."

Military barriers
(Atomegorodok, silence
comrade!—

Intellectual barriers
(Berkeley, far out
brother!—

separating the others
from the common mortals

The great message coming from there, send it

just like old times! Via Air Mail

—May My China in reverse go ever forward

— . . . Little things in large scale, which doesn't keep them from being frightening. Do business.

—Know : "枪 杆子里面出政权"

—Beikoku (　米 穀　) wo busō (　武裝　) to Kaeru
　　(exchange rice for armaments)

—Then exchange b(l)ows. . .

— . . . and handshakes with honorable precious (stamped) paper
　　tiger.　　Meet, make an ami in Miami. . . .

—Het-Chou!

الى المنف الثوري ردّا على الجريمتنا !!

Hear yourself speak of an understanding
without understanding.
         the interlocutor
Confuse the tongue with the tongue· · ·

Throw off the track! Get together at great
    exp$_e^a$nse to prepare a gratuitous
    call for peace

have for free the Boss' head on the T.V. screen

259

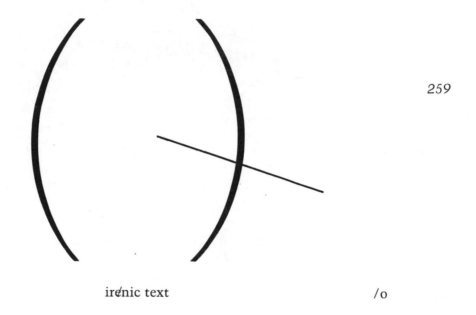

irénic text

/o

(Braille!—Watcraniumark—

imprint of writing)

260

in such a way
that it drops in right on time

BOOM

—Mama! oh, mama! . . .
—Shut up! will you . . .

—trans. Mark A. Polizzotti

19

Conclusion

The avant-garde today offers disturbed and disturbing images of the problematic situation of the individual in contemporary society. It illuminates, but does not resolve, the paradoxes of apparent personal freedom and sensed social restriction, of individual limitation and collective liberalism. As an activist art, its formal and social disruptiveness indicates the writers' unwillingness to accept the given conditions of literature and soiety. Clearly, the avant-garde no longer asserts an unbounded faith that radical change will emerge from aesthetic innovations or social institutions. Instead, this art of tentative questioning and experimentation is an art of ambivalence. The promise and limits of the avant-garde can be perceived in several conflicting interpretations of contemporary avant-garde practice. It is possible to ask alternately, as this book has done: Is the aesthetic fragmentation of character and narrative unity an expression of the diminution of individual capability in mass society? Or is it a willed, self-conscious disruption of presently inadequate means of depicting the future formulations of personal identity? Is it a sign of submission to social programming, or evidence of liberated self-creation? Is the disruption of syntax, semantic meaning, and even of word formation only an abstract, hermetic game? Or is it a means of establishing new forms of articulation? Do improvisation, gratuitousness and aleatory creative practices indicate an anarchic avoidance of the writer's responsibility to illuminate a complex social reality? Or are they effective ways of demystifying the false authority of the social superstructure? Is self-reflexive formalism a sign of acquiescence to the reactionary ideological stance of modernism? Or is the disruptive element of that self-reflexiveness a means of undermining the principles of formalism, and ultimately all semiotic authority? The answer to these questions may be that *all* positions can be maintained at the same time. In effect, the avant-garde both sustains and subverts its cultural position and promise. For, finally, it is an expression of a larger cultural ideology which contains and even fosters its own contradictions, of which one is the avant-garde.

The avant-garde today is clearly a subsidiary movement in an already limited aesthetic framework—postmodernism. Both exist within the fully acculturated tradition of high art. But by expressing its disruptive antagonism to the given practice of literature—whether popular, postmodern, or a previous avant-garde—and, by extension, by questioning the social context of this practice, the avant-garde exposes some of the contradictions of the nature of writing (including itself) in this society. The ambivalent status of the avant-garde is a sign of its being both dependent on the reigning ideologies of our culture and subversive of their hegemony. Whether this culture manages to successfully contain its internal tensions and contradictions, such as the avant-garde, of course depends on more factors than mere aesthetic innovation, though that innovation may perhaps finally have social significance.

The avant-garde, however visionary, does not exist independent of its society—a society whose underlying disquietude it articulates, but a society which has recently spawned only the most muted and problematic movements of radical change. The visionary and antagonistic dimensions of the contemporary avant-garde indicate a questioning process and a state of unfulfilled desire, but they barely begin to suggest possible solutions. Whether any social transformation is possible involves questions larger than the contemporary avant-garde, as well as its society, seems as yet willing to raise.

The focus on this anthology has been on the avant-garde *today*, since, despite its name, this avant-garde cannot claim with assurance to be in advance of anything particular. Rather, the avant-garde is a direct expression of the present moment. If its forced dynamics of innovation and discovery lead beyond themselves, the future that is ushered in will be as much a surprise to the writer as to the audience.

Notes on Authors

Alain Arias-Misson was born in Brussels in 1936 and raised in the United States. During the past two decades he has been extremely active in the visual poetry movement in Europe and the United States, as well as contributing to the development of new fiction. He published his "superfiction," *The Confessions of a Murderer, Rapist, Fascist, Bomber, Thief or a Year in the Journal of an Ordinary American* (Chicago Review Press) in 1975. Most recently, he has published a book of visual poetry, *The Public Poem Book* (Factotum Press, Italy).

Amiri Baraka, formerly Leroi Jones, is author of numerous books of poetry, including *Preface to a Twenty Volume Suicide Note*, *The Dead Lecturer*, and the recent *Hard Facts*; fiction, *The System of Dante's Hell* and *Tales*; plays, *The Dutchman*, *The Baptism*, *Four Black Revolutionary Plays*, among many others; and collections of essays, including *Home*, *Black Music*, and *Raise Race Rays Raze*. Born in Newark in 1934, he has been active in that city's political life for more than a decade.

Jürgen Becker was born in Cologne in 1932. He has worked there as an editor for publishers and radio, has written radio plays, published poetry, *Schnee* (1971), *Das Ende der Landschaftsmalerei* (1974), a book of photographic "narratives," *Eine Zeit ohne Wörter*, and several prose works, including *Felder* (1964), *Ränder* (1968), and *Umgebungen* (1970).

John Cage, born in 1912, has long been a major force in modern music, as well as an influential figure in dance and the visual arts. His essays, lectures, diaries, and recently his own creative works based on texts of Thoreau and Joyce have been published by Wesleyan University Press as *Silence* (1961), *A Year From Monday* (1966), *M.* (1973), and *Empty Words* (1979).

Marvin Cohen was born in New York in 1931 and has been an ever-present figure in and around the literary scene there since the late 1950's. His short fictions have appeared in countless little magazines; many have been collected and published in book form, along with his novels. His books include *The Self-Devoted Friend*, *The Monday Rhetoric of the Love Club*, *Baseball the Beautiful*, *Others, Including Morstive Sternbump*, and *The Inconvenience of Living*.

Charles Elwert teaches creative writing in Illinois and has published work in *Laughing Bear*, *Assembling*, and *The Paris Review*.

Raymond Federman was born in France in 1928 and has lived in the United States since World War II. He is currently a professor of English at SUNY/Buffalo and has published scholarly books on Samuel Beckett. In 1967 he published a bilingual book of poems, *Among the Beasts/Parmi les monstres*, and in 1979 a bilingual edition of *The Voice in the Closet* (Coda Press) with an essay by Maurice Roche. This handsome book should be considered the most complete version of the work. He has also written two novels in English, *Double or Nothing* (Swallow Press, 1971) and *Take It or Leave It* (Fiction Collective, 1976).

Helmut Heissenbüttel was born in 1921 in Germany. He presently lives in Stuttgart, where he has worked as a radio producer since 1959. Between 1960 and 1967 he published six volumes of experimental texts, which were collected in 1970 as *Das Textbuch*. He has also published a novel, *D'Alemberts Ende* (1970), as well as several important books of critical essays, including *Über Literatur* (1966), *Was ist das Konkrete an einem Gedicht?* (1969), and *Zur Tradition der Moderne* (1972).

Scott Helmes works in an architectural firm in St. Paul. His visual work has been shown in the Midwest and on the West Coast and has been published recently in many small magazines such as *Interstate, Context, Assembling,* and *The Paris Review.*

Ernst Jandl was born in Vienna in 1925 where he currently resides. He has spent time in England, the United States and Berlin, but has worked most frequently in Vienna where he has collaborated frequently with Fredericke Mayröcker. He is a leading representative of the concrete poetry movement and has written many sound poems, some of which have been produced on records. Besides poems, he has written radio plays. Among his many collections (mostly published by Luchterhand), the most important are *laut und luise* (1966), *sprechblasen* (1968) and *wischen möchten* (1974) from which the selections in this anthology are taken.

Ludovic Janvier was born in 1934. His first novel, *La Baigneuse,* was published in 1968. In addition to his fiction, he has written the critical work *Pour Samuel Beckett.*

Toby Lurie has made records of his sound poems as well as having published two collections of poetry, *Conversations and Constructions* and *Conversations with the Past* (Laughing Bear Press). He lives in San Francisco.

Clarence Major has published several volumes of poetry, including *Swallow the Lake, The Cotton Club* and *The Syncopated Cakewalk,* has edited the important anthology *The New Black Poetry,* and, in addition to works of non-fiction, has published four novels, *All-Night Visitors, NO, Reflex and Bone Structure,* and *Emergency Exit,* the latter two with the Fiction Collective. The passages in this anthology appeared in different form and order in *Emergency Exit.*

Lucia Marcucci is from Florence and is a member of the "Group 70." She has had numerous exhibitions of her work in Europe and has published several books.

Friederike Mayröcker was born in 1924 in Vienna. Her experimental works appear as prose, verse, drama and radio plays. Her books of poetry include *meta-phorisch* (1965), *Texte* (1966) and *In langsamen Blitzen* (1974). The pieces in this collection come from her book of stories *Je ein umwölkter Gipfel* (1973).

Eugenio Miccini was born in 1925 in Florence where he has been active in the avant-garde poetry movements as director of the *Techne* center and a member of the "Group 63" and "Group 70."

Luciano Ori was born in 1928, also in Florence, and is a co-founder of the "Group 70." He has published ten books of poetry, several plays and numerous critical and theoretical articles on visual poetry. In addition, his works have been widely exhibited throughout Europe.

Maurice Roche has published, in addition to *CodeX*, three other novels, *Compact*, *Circus* and *Opéra Bouffe*, all with Éditions du Seuil.

Gerhard Rühm was born in Vienna in 1930. Though he originally studied composition, since 1953, when he formed the experimental "Wiener Gruppe" with H. C. Artmann and Konrad Bayer, he has devoted most of his energy to literature. Visual poetry is his main interest, but he has also written sound poems, dialect poems, prose, plays and made records. His main collections are *fenster* (prose, 1968), *Gesammelte Gedichte und visuelle Texte* (1970) and *Ophelia und die Wörter* (theater, 1972).

Severo Sarduy was born in Cuba in 1937 where he began writing both before and after the revolution. In the mid-sixties, he left Cuba for Madrid, then Paris, to study art history. Since 1965 he has been associated with *Tel Quel*. His first novel, *Gestos*, was written as a form of "action writing" inspired by the paintings of Franz Kline. His second novel, *De donde son los cantantes* (1967) appeared as *From Cuba with a Song* in the book *Triple Cross* (Dutton, 1972). His next novel was *Cobra* (1972). *Maitreya* was first published in 1977.

Shimizu Toshihiko is active in the VOU group in Tokyo where he has had numerous exhibitions of his work. His books include *Once Again* (New Directions, 1964).

Philippe Sollers is a novelist, critic and editor of *Tel Quel*. For the past two decades, he has been a major voice in French letters. His most important innovative novels include *Drame, Lois, Nombres* and *H*.

Takahashi Shohachiro lives in Morioka, Japan. He is active in the VOU group as well as the ASA group in Tokyo and is co-founder of *317*, a visual poetry magazine.

269

Jiri Valoch lives in Brno, Czechoslovakia and has published in many Western Europe publications, in addition to frequently exhibiting his work.

Paul de Vree lives in Antwerp where he is editor of *Tafelronde*. He was a co-founder of the visual and experimental poetry magazine *Lotta Poetica* (Brescia, Italy) and Factotum Books (Padua, Italy).

Note on the Editor

Charles Russell teaches in the English Department at
Rutgers University, Newark. He is Executive Editor of
The American Book Review and an Associate Editor of
The Paris Review.